Low- Cholesterol Jewish Cookery

Low~Cholesterol Jewish Cookery

June Roth

ARCO PUBLISHING COMPANY, INC.
219 Park Avenue South, New York, N.Y. 10003

Published 1978 by Arco Publishing Company, Inc.
219 Park Avenue South, New York, N.Y. 10003

Copyright © 1972 by June Roth

Library of Congress Cataloging in Publication Data

Roth, June Spiewak.
  Low-cholesterol Jewish cookery.

  First published in 1972 under title: Healthier Jewish
cookery.
  Includes index.
  1. Cookery, Jewish.   2. Low-cholesterol diet.
I. Title.
TX724.R588   1978   641.5'63   77-13968
ISBN 0-668-04420-9

Printed in the United States of America

IN FOND MEMORY OF FRED'S BELOVED BABU,
DEAR MAMA LAURA, AND GENTLE PAPA JOE

Contents

)❖))❖

Foreword

)◆

In the process of bringing exquisite taste sensations and gourmet delights to its devotees over the years, Jewish cooking has possibly shortened more lives than several fair-sized pogroms. Traditionally made chicken soup with its high content of chicken fat has been affectionately but sadly mislabeled "Jewish Penicillin" for its supposed healing properties. Aside from its psychological and liquid caloric benefits, it is to predisposed individuals a cholesterol time bomb set to go off at some later but not-late-enough date.

There is enough "hard" and "soft" data available today to have convinced most medical scientists and researchers in the field that the "great plague" of the twentieth century, coronary artery disease and atherosclerosis, is at least partially due to a diet high in saturated fats. Among the "soft" data is the long-known fact that older orthodox Jewish men far more frequently develop advanced atherosclerosis of the coronary arteries and the lower aorta. Many years ago the latter was called "synagogue disease" because it was thought to be brought about by sitting many hours a day in a temple of worship and rocking while praying. I learned, also, more than 30 years ago, that I could look all the way down an open 40 bed ward of male cardiac patients at predominately black Harlem Hospital in New York City and from the doorway diagnose the two whites as "coronaries, Jewish, and local shopkeepers." The other 38 patients were always hypertensive, rheumatic, luetic, or other types of heart patients. Incidentally, this method of diagnosis would fail miserably today! Therapeutic medicine has improved and lessened some of the black man's cardiac problems while his changed and "improved" eating habits have added coronary disease to his list of troubles.

The problem of retaining the really great pleasures of a fine culinary art while removing its serious potential for harm has been tackled courageously and capably by the author of this book. It is interesting to note that the federal government is sponsoring a large-scale preliminary trial to obtain final confirmation of the value of a solution such as this book offers. In this controlled study, now about in its third year, all food is furnished to the 5000 or so male participants. Half of them unknowingly get what looks and tastes like high-saturated fat foods but which are actually made with unsaturated fats. If the results of this study are encouraging, in terms of fewer coronaries and less vascular disease, it will be expanded to one or two million people! If the final results are sufficiently conclusive, the eating habits of this country will then probably be drastically "influenced" by government edict.

This book therefore anticipates and serves a beginning trend which I predict will result in tremendous changes in the content and composition of foodstuffs in the next 25 years. It is not necessary to wait for final and irrefutable proof. The handwriting is already on the wall. When the full beneficial results of these dietary changes are felt in the first half of the 21st century, the medical scientists of that day will stroke their retrospective beards and confirm what we more than suspect; namely that in this era an unfortuitous combination of evoluted habits and mores of poor diet plus automated and electronic sloth and smoking produced a disastrous "coronary epidemic."

Most change, particularly for good, is traumatic. Congratulations to the author for showing us an easy, non-traumatic way to have your schmalz unsaturated and live and be well!

S. K. FINEBERG, M.D., F.A.C.P., F.(A)A.C.C.
Clinical Ass't Prof. of Medicine,
New York Medical College
Chief, Diabetes and Obesity—Diabetes
Clinics, Metropolitan Hosp., N.Y.C.
Director of Medicine and Cardiologist,
Prospect Hospital, Bronx, N.Y.

Low-Cholesterol Jewish Cookery

1. How to Reform Traditional Cooking

꒰꜀꜀꜀꜀꜀꜀꜀꜀꜀꜀꜀꜀꜀꜀꜀꜀꜀꜀꜀꜀꜀꜀꜀꜀꜀꜀꜀꜀꜀꜀꜀꜀꜀꜀

Jewish cuisine ranks high among the tastiest forms of culinary arts known to the world. It should . . . because it reflects the best cooking techniques of the geographical areas in which the Jewish people made their homes.

These methods were adapted to the dietary laws of the religion, and show us the availability of ingredients in each area of the world. Recipes that have been handed down from mother to daughter are still being practiced today with much the same procedures and ingredients as great-grandmothers used to prepare the traditional dishes of their families.

For some, the time has come to reconsider those recipes. Atherosclerosis is considered to be due to a combination of factors. It is the cause of premature heart attacks . . . the leading killer in this country. One of the factors leading to atherosclerosis is the body's own manufacture of high levels of cholesterol in the bloodstream, generally thought to be caused partly by consuming large amounts

1

of animal fats rather than vegetable fats. It would make good sense, then, to try to limit the body's intake of necessary fats to those that are unsaturated and free of the guilt of contributing to the development of atherosclerosis . . . particularly to those people who may also have some of the other contributing factors that lead to this disease.

The American Heart Association warns of a combination of:

High blood pressure
High levels of cholesterol
Overweight
Excessive eating
Too little exercise
Diabetes
Excessive cigarette smoking
Tensions and stresses
Heredity

This presents a problem to those who must, for health reasons, cut down drastically on the use of saturated fats such as butter, whole milk, cream, eggs, and animal fats. They are told to substitute the unsaturated fats that are obtained from vegetable products. Many people, who are so instructed by their doctors, find it difficult to adapt their heritage of recipes to the strict rules of unsaturated-fat cooking. They don't know when they may substitute yoghurt made of skim milk for that dearly beloved sour cream, corn oil margarine for butter, vegetable oils for overused chicken fat, or new simmering techniques for the old hand-me-down frying methods.

What will happen to chopped chicken livers if they must be cooked without a generous dose of rendered chicken fat to give them the creamy consistency that makes one salivate with food memories? You won't even miss the old way if you use the recipe in this book!

How can matzo knaidlach be made for Passover without adding some chicken fat to the batter before forming those soup-floating delights? The only thing missing will be the traditional heartburn, avoided by using forethought!

Will it be worth the effort to make the change from saturated cooking to unsaturated cooking? You can BET YOUR LIFE it will!

The recipes in this book have been devised to give you the old-fashioned tastes in a healthier way. They make lavish use of herbs and spices that have been lost in the hand-me-down recipes that were often word-of-mouth or simple "watch me" directions. These seasonings were often eliminated from the recipe by the ancestor who refused to share her secret way of making traditional dishes. Many times the bits of taste tantalizers just disappeared from the recipe as it was handed on to others.

Now the herbs and spices are back . . . and the saturated fats are heading for oblivion . . . as you use this treasury of traditional recipes that combine dietary laws and doctor's orders for healthier eating.

2. Appetizers and Cocktail Offerings

))•

You're off to a healthier start when you plan to use one of these imaginative first course recipes! Several traditional Jewish dishes show new techniques to earn their poly-unsaturated medal of honor. Try them and see if the wise old taste buds in your family can sense anything but improvement, while you alone know you are safeguarding those you love. This is one time when action certainly speaks louder than words!

))•))

You will find this to be a healthy departure from the time-honored method of sautéing the chicken livers in chicken fat and then saturating the chopped liver with more chicken fat to hold it together. The method below simmers the livers and onion together in water until just cooked and delicately soft. Then it is chopped or ground with eggs. This streamlines about 400 calories of saturated animal fat right out, to say nothing of the repeat performance problem with dark-fried onions and hard-cooked livers!

CHOPPED CHICKEN LIVERS

1 pound fresh chicken livers
1 onion, sliced thin
2 hard-cooked eggs
¼ teaspoon salt
⅛ teaspoon pepper

Place chicken livers and sliced onion rings in a large skillet; barely cover the bottom of the skillet with water. Cover and simmer for five minutes, turning the livers occasionally and adding more water if needed to keep livers from sticking to the pan. Chop or grind livers, onions, and hard-cooked eggs together; stir in just enough pan juices to hold the mixture together. Add salt and pepper; chill until ready to use. Serve as a spread with crackers, as a first course, or as a luncheon salad. Makes about 1½ cups of chopped liver.

)✦)

Peanut butter is the secret ingredient that binds this "mock chopped liver" into a tasty imitation. The trick is to grind it very fine!

MOCK CHOPPED LIVER

2 onions, diced
2 tablespoons peanut oil
¼ small head cabbage
2 carrots, scraped

1 stalk celery, trimmed
1 small green pepper, seeded
3 tablespoons peanut butter
¼ teaspoon salt
⅛ teaspoon pepper

Sauté onions in peanut oil until just golden. Grind (with a fine blade) the cabbage, carrots, celery, and green pepper. Add sautéed onions through the grinder. Stir in peanut butter, salt, and pepper; mix very well. Serve as a spread for crackers, or in scoops on lettuce. Makes about 1½ cups.

))✦))

Chopped eggplant has long been a staple appetizer and spread. Here it is baked, rather than fried, to prevent the eggplant's natural tendency to soak up oil like a sponge. Then just chop and season as directed!

CHOPPED EGGPLANT

1 medium eggplant
1 small onion, diced
2 tablespoons lemon juice
¾ teaspoon salt
¼ teaspoon pepper
1 teaspoon sugar
1 tablespoon peanut oil

Bake the whole eggplant, uncovered, in a 350°F. oven until the skin turns dark brown and is wrinkled. Remove from oven, cut the skin away, and then cut eggplant into several thick manageable slices. Place these in a large chopping bowl, add the onion, and chop together until it is all very fine. Add the lemon juice, salt, pepper, and sugar; stir well. Then add the peanut oil and stir again. Chill. Serve with thin slices of dark bread or tiny party rye slices. Makes about 2 cups of spread.

)❖)

Mayonnaise is made with eggs and oil, so to cut down on the amount of egg involved, the dressing here consists of part mayonnaise and part skim milk yoghurt. Just fine to start a dairy meal.

HERRING SALAD

4 hard-cooked eggs
¼ cup vinegar
3 herring, cleaned and picked in pieces
3 cups coarsely chopped apple
2½ cups cubed boiled potato
¼ cup mayonnaise
¼ cup yoghurt
½ cup mixed nuts, chopped
½ cup chopped dill pickle
¼ cup chopped onion
¼ cup sugar
Dash pepper

Mash egg yolks with vinegar; chop egg whites fine. Mix yolk mixture and chopped egg whites with remaining ingredients. Chill. Makes 8 to 10 servings.

)❖)

This is to serve on an otherwise eggless day, if a heart patient is involved. It divides up to give each consumer just a part of an egg, and a good deal of delicious sardine salad.

CHOPPED SARDINE SALAD

2 3¾-ounce cans sardines, drained and broken in pieces
2 hard-cooked eggs, chopped
¼ cup chopped onion
2 tablespoons mayonnaise
2 tablespoons yoghurt
2 tablespoons vinegar
1½ tablespoons sugar

Mix the sardines, egg, and onion together. Stir the mayonnaise, yoghurt, vinegar and sugar together; add this mixture to the sardine mixture and stir. Chill for several hours. Serve as an appetizer or sandwich filling. Makes 1⅔ cups.

꘎

Instead of frying these mushrooms in fat the usual way, here is a method of simmering them in broth and then thickening the sauce. The Worcestershire sauce gives both tang and color!

SLICED MUSHROOMS ON TOAST POINTS

½ pound sliced fresh mushrooms
2 stalks fresh celery, sliced
1 small onion, sliced thin
1 cup broth
½ teaspoon paprika
1 teaspoon Worcestershire sauce
1 teaspoon cornstarch
3 slices toast, cut diagonally

Place sliced mushrooms, celery, and onion in a skillet. Add broth, paprika, and Worcestershire sauce. Simmer slowly until vegetables are soft. Stir cornstarch with just enough water to make a thin paste; add some of the broth from the skillet to this paste and return the entire mixture to the skillet. Stir constantly until the mixture thickens. Spoon at once onto toast halves. Makes 6 servings.

)❧)

Stuff these mushroom caps with tuna and flavor with soy sauce and sesame seeds. A pinch of ginger snaps it up to guest level!

MUSHROOM TIDBITS

1 7-ounce can water-packed tuna, drained and flaked
2 tablespoons mayonnaise
2 tablespoons yoghurt
3 tablespoons chopped watercress (optional)
1 tablespoon sesame seeds
1 tablespoon soy sauce
½ teaspoon ground ginger
24 quarter-size mushroom caps (stems removed)

Mix together the tuna, mayonnaise, yoghurt, watercress, sesame seeds, soy sauce, and ginger. Stuff each mushroom cap with generous quantity of tuna mixture. Place on a broiling tray and broil for several minutes. Serve hot. Makes 24 hors d'oeuvres.

)❧)

From Italy comes the idea of serving a tray of tidbits to be passed around the table. But the ingredients are a happy blending of favored appetizers in Jewish cooking.

ANTIPASTO TRAY

1 cup herring in wine sauce, cut up
8 slices salami
1 6-ounce jar pickled artichoke hearts
1 cup whole cherry tomatoes
1 1-pound jar pickled beets and onions
Lettuce cups

Arrange each ingredient on a lettuce cup and set on a suitable tray. Each person then spoons some of each ingredient onto his own appetizer plate. Makes 4 to 6 servings.

꣒꣒

For another dairy meal starter, try this tuna-cottage cheese spread. Horseradish and capers are the uncommon pick-me-up for an otherwise bland mixture!

TUNA CHEESE SPREAD

1 7-ounce can water-packed tuna, drained and flaked
¼ cup cottage cheese
2 tablespoons mayonnaise
2 tablespoons yoghurt
2 tablespoons finely chopped onion
1 teaspoon horseradish
½ teaspoon chopped capers (optional)
¼ teaspoon Worcestershire sauce
Melba toast rounds or crackers

Mix the tuna and cottage cheese together. Add mayonnaise, yoghurt, onion, horseradish, capers, and Worcestershire sauce. Mix well. Chill. Spread on crackers or place in a bowl for do-it-yourself spreading. Makes 1½ cups or enough for 36 crackers.

)♦)

Avocados have a subtle flavor, and in this dip that flavor is brought out. Use it for dipping fresh cauliflower buds, carrot spears, or celery chunks, for a wonderful lo-cal beginner.

AVOCADO DIP

2 ripe avocados
1 tomato, skinned
1 small onion, minced
2 tablespoons wine vinegar
1 teaspoon salt
¼ teaspoon pepper

Peel and mash the avocados. Mince the tomato and add to avocado; add onion. Stir all together and add vinegar, salt, and pepper. Cover tightly and refrigerate until ready to serve. Serve with crackers and prepared fresh vegetable spears. Makes about 1 cup of dip.

)♦)

Broiled grapefruit tastes nothing like the cold variety, and this version has a touch of honey to make it very special. A glamour way of serving a nutritious fruit!

HONEY–BROILED GRAPEFRUIT

2 seedless grapefruits
4 tablespoons honey

Cut each grapefruit in half and spread each cut side

with 1 tablespoon of honey. Broil for 10 minutes or until lightly browned. Serve at once. Makes 4 servings.

)▷◆)▶

Although this fresh fruit ambrosia is presented as an appetizer, it would make an equally welcome dessert. Flaked coconut makes it very special!

FRESH FRUIT AMBROSIA

3 grapefruits
3 oranges
1 cup fresh strawberries, sliced
3 tablespoons sugar
¼ cup flaked coconut

Chill oranges and grapefruits before preparing. Cut slice from top, then cut off peel in strips from top to bottom, cutting deep enough to remove white membrane. Then cut slice from bottom. Go over fruit again, removing any remaining white membrane. Section grapefruits and 2 of the oranges by cutting along side of each dividing membrane from outside to middle of core. Remove section by section, over bowl, to retain juice. Slice remaining orange crosswise, ¼ inch thick. Combine grapefruit, oranges and strawberries; sprinkle with sugar. Turn into serving bowl or individual dishes and sprinkle with coconut. Makes 6 servings.

)▷◆)▶

In this recipe the orange shells become the serving cup, and all is baked together with a fluffy mystery topping. It's bound to become a favorite at your house!

BAKED AMBROSIA

3 oranges
¼ cup pitted dates
2 tablespoons coconut
½ cup chopped walnuts
½ cup plain yoghurt
½ teaspoon vanilla

Cut oranges in half and scoop out the fruit, leaving the half-shells intact. Chop dates and mix with cut-up orange pulp. Add coconut and chopped walnuts. Spoon into the orange shells and place in a baking dish. Bake for 25 minutes in a 350°F. oven. Remove from oven. Stir yoghurt and vanilla together, beating a little to make the mixture fluffy. Spoon some on top of each baked orange. Serve at once. Makes 6 servings.

꒦꒧꒦

Plain stewed prunes have a devoted following, but once you try them with apricot brandy you'll be serving them quite often. This method keeps the flavor from cooking out of the fruit!

BRANDIED PRUNES

1 one-pound package large dried prunes
½ cup boiling water
¼ cup apricot brandy

Empty prunes into a jar with tight-fitting lid; add boiling water and shake several times after lid is in place. Let prunes sit at room temperature for several hours. Then add apricot brandy, mix thoroughly, and chill until ready to serve. Makes 6 to 8 servings.

)❖)

Kadota figs take on a brand new appearance with the addition of snipped apricots and walnut halves. And so easy to prepare this tangy treat!

KADOTA FIG CUP

2 cups canned Kadota figs with juice
½ cup snipped dried apricots
½ cup walnut halves

Place figs and juice in a small bowl with snipped dried apricots. Chill. To serve, spoon into 6 sherbet glasses and top with walnut halves. Makes 6 servings.

)❖)

Just a flick of the can opener turns you into an inventive cook, and this fruit and nut appetizer is a sure palate-pleaser. Pretty glasses do enhance the offering!

MANDARIN–PEACH CUP

1 11-ounce can mandarin oranges
1 16-ounce can sliced peaches
1 15½-ounce can crushed pineapple
3 tablespoons slivered almonds

Combine oranges, peaches, and crushed pineapple. Spoon into eight sherbet glasses and chill. Top with a teaspoon of slivered almonds each. Makes 8 servings.

)❖)

As soon as you have peeled and diced the fresh pears for this fruit cup, combine them with the crushed pineapple and juice to prevent discoloration. And while the flavors are mingling you can perk up the color with bright red cherries!

PEAR–PINEAPPLE CUP

2 fresh pears, peeled and diced
1 20-ounce can crushed pineapple
1 cup maraschino cherries, cut in half

Combine diced pears, crushed pineapple (including juice) and maraschino cherries. Spoon into 6 sherbet glasses and chill. Makes 6 servings.

)❖)

The sweetness of the wine used in this fruit combination helps to balance the tartness of the fresh ingredients. Makes it seem a little more special too!

FRESH FRUIT AND WINE CUP

1 apple
1 orange
1 cup seedless grapes
½ cup Concord grape wine

Leave skin on apple and dice. Peel orange and cut in sections. Combine apple and orange with seedless grapes; pour wine over all. Spoon into 6 sherbet glasses. Chill and serve. Makes 6 servings.

)❖)

You won't even miss sour cream with your strawberries if you follow this blender trick with extra berries and yoghurt. If you pile all into stemmed glassware it will be elegant enough for dessert!

STRAWBERRY CUP

1 pint fresh strawberries
1 cup vanilla yoghurt
1 tablespoon confectioners' sugar

Wash and hull strawberries; reserve ½ cup soft or less attractive berries. Pile remaining whole berries into 6 sherbet glasses. Put reserved berries, yoghurt, and confectioners' sugar into an electric blender; blend on high for a moment and pour mixture over the whole berries. Chill and serve. Makes 6 servings.

)❖)

This combination is bound to stir up conversation, as the pineapple chunks take on the pink color of the spiced apple syrup. Makes an interesting side dish to a meat course too!

PINEAPPLE COMPOTE

1 20-ounce can pineapple chunks
1 14-ounce jar spiced sliced apples

Drain pineapple chunks and reserve syrup for another use. While spiced apples are still in the jar, cut into chunks with a sharp knife. Combine the spiced apples and syrup with the drained pineapple chunks. Chill until pineapple chunks turn pink from the syrup. Makes 8 servings.

)❖)

These fresh fruits get along swimmingly with a splash of ice-cold bubbling lemon beverage. Use lo-cal if you're cutting calories!

SUMMER FRESH MELON CUP

1 cup cantaloupe melon balls
1 cup honeydew melon balls
1 cup fresh cherries, pitted
1 cup low-calorie carbonated lemon beverage

Spoon melon balls and cherries into 6 sherbet glasses. Chill. Just before serving, splash each with chilled lemon beverage. Makes 6 servings.

)✦)

Want to serve melon a different way? Here's a method of using the melon itself as the gelatin mold!

GELATIN FILLED MELON

1 honeydew melon
1 3-ounce package lime gelatin
1 cup boiling water
1 9-ounce can fruit cocktail

Cut top off melon and scoop out all the seeds. Empty gelatin into a bowl and dissolve with boiling water. Drain juice from fruit cocktail into a measuring cup and add water until it measures ¾ cup of liquid. Add to gelatin and mix thoroughly. Add fruit salad. Pour this mixture into the melon cavity (if you prop the melon into a deep bowl, it will be easier to do), and top with cut piece of melon. Chill for several hours until gelatin is solid. When ready to serve, cut crosswise into melon rings with gelatin centers. Makes 8 servings.

)✦)

3. Nourishing Soups

)✦

Join the back-to-nature movement and make your own pot of soup. These have been carefully devised to get the most flavor and the least fat for your money. Do add the herbs and spices called for to get real old-fashioned sensations!

)✦)

10/31/81 - ½ rec

Added -
1 bay leaf
1 clove
4 peppercorns
sprinklg of dillweed

Although chicken soup has gained fame as a cure-all that mama used to spoon-feed to the sick, it was actually floating with fat and heavily salted. Here's how to change a lethal dose into the loving care it was meant to be!

CHICKEN SOUP

1 chicken, preferably fowl, about 4 pounds
2 quarts water
2 large onions

Several stalks of celery, including leaves
Several scraped carrots
3 sprigs parsley
3 sprigs fresh dill
1 teaspoon salt
→1 teaspoon sugar

Place chicken in a deep pot and cover with water. Add neck, gizzard, and even feet if you have them. Add onions, peeled and whole, celery, and carrots. Add parsley and dill. Season with salt and sugar. Bring to a boil and then turn the heat low and simmer for 1½ to 2 hours, covered. Remove chicken from the soup. Pour soup through a strainer into a large clean container; rescue the whole carrots and add them to the soup, discarding the rest of the vegetables and herbs. Refrigerate the soup until the fat rises and solidifies enough to be easily removed. Heat when ready to serve and garnish each serving with noodles, a piece of carrot, and a matzo ball made the healthier way (page 35). Makes 8 to 10 servings.

))✦))

Chicken soup can wear other masks too! Here it parades as a flavorful onion soup. Just double the Worcestershire sauce if you prefer it dark and spicy.

ONION SOUP

10/31/81 - ½ rec.
Added 1 bay leaf
1 clove
4 peppercorns

1 quart chicken soup
4 large onions, sliced thin
¼ teaspoon Worcestershire sauce
6 slices toasted Italian bread

Pour chicken soup into a large saucepan; add onions and Worcestershire sauce. Simmer, covered, for 20 minutes, or until onions are soft. Serve topped with a slice of toasted bread. Makes 6 servings.

))•◦))

This vegetable soup is a meal in itself, if you decide to serve the chunks of meat right in the bowl. Otherwise, use the soup meat as part of your main course. Either way, it will be a treat!

VEGETABLE SOUP

2 pounds beef flanken
2 quarts water
1 one-pound can tomatoes
1 large onion, diced
2 stalks celery, diced
4 carrots, sliced thin
½ pound peas, shelled
½ pound green beans, sliced
2 tablespoons rice
1½ teaspoons salt
¼ teaspoon pepper
¼ teaspoon basil

Place beef in a heavy saucepan and add water. Simmer for 1 hour, skimming off the surface as it cooks. Add tomatoes, onion, celery, and carrots, and cook for 15 minutes more. Add peas, green beans, rice, salt, pepper, and basil. Cook for 30 minutes more. Remove beef and serve it separately, or cut in chunks and serve it in the soup. Makes 10 to 12 servings.

))•◦))

An easy way to peel the beets for this borscht is to "blanch" them first . . . plunge them into rapidly boiling water for a minute, and then into ice water. The skins will slip off easily!

BORSCHT - *chilled*

2 bunches beets
2 quarts water
Juice of 1 lemon
→ 3 tablespoons sugar
¼ teaspoon salt

Peel and slice beets thin. Place in a heavy saucepan with water. Add lemon juice, sugar, and salt. Bring to a boil; reduce heat and cover. Simmer for 1 hour. Serve chilled with chopped cucumber or a hot boiled potato. Makes 10 to 12 servings.

❧

Perhaps you know this sorrel soup by its other name of "schav." To many it is an alternate selection with borscht. With both it's important to get the right balance of sweet and sour!

SORREL SOUP - *chilled*

2 cups chopped sorrel leaves
1 small onion, sliced
2 tablespoons corn oil margarine
6 cups water
½ teaspoon salt
¼ teaspoon cayenne
1 tablespoon lemon juice
→ 1 tablespoon sugar
1 egg

Cook sorrel and onion in margarine until limp; then add water, salt, cayenne, lemon juice, and sugar. Bring to a boil, reduce heat and simmer for 35 minutes. Strain. Beat egg, and slowly pour into the sorrel soup while stirring constantly to prevent curdling. Chill. Serve cold with a dollop of plain yoghurt, if desired. Makes 6 to 8 servings.

Ⅱ✦Ⅱ

The following recipe is the dairy version of mushroom-barley soup. If dietary rules prevail and a non-dairy soup is preferred, substitute water for skim milk in the last stage of preparation.

MUSHROOM–BARLEY SOUP

½ pound sliced fresh mushrooms
¼ cup barley
1 onion, diced
1 carrot, scraped and diced fine
1 quart water
A few sprigs of dill, minced
1½ teaspoons salt
¼ teaspoon pepper
2 tablespoons flour
1 cup skim milk

Put mushrooms, barley, onion, and carrot into a heavy saucepan. Add water, dill, salt, and pepper. Bring to a boil, reduce heat and cover; simmer for 1 hour. Stir flour into milk and mix until well-blended. Gradually add to soup, stirring constantly. Let soup thicken a bit and serve hot. Makes 6 servings.

Ⅱ✦Ⅱ

This hearty peasant soup will stick-to-your-ribs and be worth all the effort to prepare. Here again, the balance of sweet and sour is of prime importance!

SWEET AND SOUR CABBAGE SOUP

2 or 3 soup bones
1 head of cabbage, shredded
1½ quarts water
1 one-pound can tomatoes
2 onions, sliced thin
1 apple, peeled and diced
¼ cup seedless raisins
¼ cup lemon juice
¼ cup brown sugar
1 teaspoon salt
¼ teaspoon pepper

Put the soup bones in a heavy saucepan. Add the shredded cabbage and water. Add the tomatoes, onions, apple, and raisins. Add the lemon juice, brown sugar, salt and pepper. Stir. Bring to a boil, reduce heat and simmer for 1½ hours, stirring occasionally. Makes 6 to 8 servings.

)›‹)

This is a soup to create a clamor for second helpings, so don't hesitate to double the ingredients and be prepared!

TOMATO SOUP

2 meaty beef neck bones
1 28-ounce can tomatoes
3 cups water
3 tablespoons rice
1 onion, diced

→ 1 teaspoon sugar
½ teaspoon salt
¼ teaspoon pepper
¼ teaspoon basil

Place neck bones in a heavy saucepan. Add tomatoes, water, rice and onion. Stir. Add sugar, salt, pepper, and basil. Bring to a boil, reduce heat, cover and simmer for 2 hours. Stir occasionally. Serve with bits of neck meat. Makes 6 servings.

꩜

Here's a little more work than opening a can to get good cream of tomato soup. Try it and you may learn to become soup chef of the year!

CREAMED TOMATO SOUP

1 one-pound can tomatoes
1 small onion, sliced
1 sprig parsley
1 bay leaf
3 cloves
1 teaspoon salt
¼ teaspoon cayenne
1 teaspoon Worcestershire sauce
4 cups water
3 tablespoons corn oil margarine
3 tablespoons flour

Empty tomatoes into a saucepan. Add sliced onion, parsley, bay leaf, cloves, salt, cayenne, Worcestershire sauce, and water. Cook for 20 minutes. Press through a sieve or food mill. Melt margarine in a small saucepan; add flour and stir until smooth. Pour some of the tomato soup into the margarine-flour mixture, and stir until very smooth; then gradually return this mixture to the tomato soup, stirring constantly. Heat and stir for several minutes before serving. Makes 6 servings.

꩜

This soup can also double as a main course, or be easily followed by a vegetable platter. Thick slices of fresh bread will enhance it either way!

FISH CHOWDER

1½ pounds fillet of haddock, flounder, or cod
1 large onion, diced
2 large potatoes, diced
2 stalks celery, diced fine
1 quart skim milk
2 tablespoons corn oil margarine
½ teaspoon salt
¼ teaspoon pepper
¼ teaspoon thyme
2 tablespoons cornstarch

Place fish in a large saucepan; cover with water and cook until fish falls apart easily. Add onion, potatoes, and celery, and simmer until they are tender. Add milk, margarine, salt, pepper, and thyme. Simmer and stir until margarine is melted. Stir cornstarch with just enough water to make a smooth thin paste; spoon some of the hot soup liquid into this paste and then return the entire mixture to the soup, stirring constantly. Continue to stir and cook until soup thickens slightly. Then serve at once. Makes 8 to 10 servings.

⊃❂⊃

Hot, this soup has a peasant background. But cold, and electric blended into a thick puree, it becomes an elegant vichyssoise!

POTATO SOUP - *hot or cold*

3 large potatoes, diced
1 leek or small onion, diced fine
2 stalks celery, diced fine
½ teaspoon salt
⅛ teaspoon pepper
½ teaspoon dried dillweed
1 quart skim milk
2 tablespoons corn oil margarine
2 tablespoons cornstarch

Put diced potato, leek or onion, celery, salt, pepper, and dillweed in a large saucepan; barely cover with water and cook until potatoes are soft. Add milk and margarine; simmer and stir until margarine is melted. Stir cornstarch with just enough water to make a smooth thin paste; spoon some of the hot soup liquid into this paste and then return the entire mixture to the soup, stirring constantly. Continue to stir and cook until soup thickens; do not let it boil. Makes 8 servings.

⊃❂⊃

If you prefer to make this soup with fresh corn, just electric blend 2 cups of cooked kernels with 1 cup of the skim milk and use in place of the can of creamed corn. Either way it will be delicious!

CREAMED CORN SOUP

1 one-pound can creamed corn *or 2 c cooked kernels*
3 cups skim milk
1½ tablespoons corn oil margarine
¾ teaspoon salt
⅛ teaspoon pepper

Empty can of creamed corn into a saucepan; add skim milk and margarine. Heat and stir for 10 minutes, until margarine is melted and mixture is piping hot; do not let it boil. Add salt and pepper. Serve at once. Makes 6 servings.

:)►:)

When it's time for a bland and subtle soup, try this fresh celery soup to make a memorable dairy meal. If more tang is desired, top with chopped chives just before serving!

CREAM OF CELERY SOUP

6/80 – Would be delicious exc for cayenne – My cayenne must have strengthened ō aging.

1 bunch celery
1 quart water
1 onion, diced fine
1 teaspoon salt
¼ teaspoon nutmeg
¼ teaspoon celery salt
¼ teaspoon cayenne *– too much*
3 tablespoons corn oil margarine
3 tablespoons flour
2 cups skim milk

Chop celery fine, after trimming well. Place in a deep saucepan; add water, onion, salt, nutmeg, celery salt, and cayenne. Bring to a boil, then reduce heat and simmer until celery and onion are soft and tender. Melt margarine; stir in flour, and then milk. Cook for several minutes, stirring constantly. Stir this mixture into the celery mixture and simmer for 5 minutes, stirring until smooth. Makes 8 to 10 servings.

)◆)

Try not to short-cut on soaking time. It makes all the difference in cooking dried lima beans!

CREAMED LIMA BEAN SOUP

1 cup dried lima beans
4 cups cold water
1 cup canned tomatoes
1 small onion, diced
1 sprig fresh parsley
1 carrot, scraped and diced
½ teaspoon salt
¼ teaspoon pepper
4 tablespoons corn oil margarine
2 tablespoons flour
3 cups skim milk
1 teaspoon Worcestershire sauce

Soak lima beans overnight, covered with cold water. Pour off water. Place beans in a heavy saucepan and add 4 cups fresh cold water. Add tomatoes, onion, parsley, carrot, salt and pepper. Cook until beans are mushy; then force bean mixture through a sieve or food mill; discard residue. In a small saucepan, melt margarine. Stir in flour and then skim milk; cook and stir constantly until mixture thickens. Add Worcestershire sauce. Pour into bean soup and heat together, stirring until smooth and creamy. Makes 6 to 8 servings.

꘎꘎

It's a good idea to save any kind of meat bones in a plastic bag in the freezer. Then when it's soup-making time, you can just remove what you need and proceed with the directions!

SPLIT PEA SOUP

2 cups split peas
2 quarts water
2 meaty beef neck bones
1 onion, diced
2 carrots, scraped and diced fine
2 stalks celery, diced fine
Several sprigs of parsley, minced
Several sprigs of fresh dill, minced
¾ teaspoon salt
¼ teaspoon pepper

Place split peas in a heavy saucepan and add water. Add remaining ingredients and stir. Bring to a boil, then turn the heat low, cover and simmer for 2½ to 3 hours. Stir occasionally. To serve, remove bones and strain through a food mill if smooth soup is desired. Otherwise serve as it is with bits of meat from the bones. Makes 8 servings.

꘎꘎

How can you stretch one small can of salmon to feed 6 to 8 people? By making the following salmon bisque of course!

SALMON BISQUE

2 tablespoons corn oil margarine
2 tablespoons flour

3 cups skim milk
1 7-ounce can salmon
¼ cup cooked peas
½ teaspoon salt
⅛ teaspoon pepper
⅛ teaspoon dillweed

Melt margarine in the bottom of a saucepan and stir in flour; blend smoothly. Then gradually stir in milk while stirring constantly; let this mixture thicken. Remove bones and skin from salmon and force it through a food mill with the peas into the milk. Add salt, pepper, and dillweed. Heat but do not boil. Makes 6 to 8 servings.

))✧))

This is a meatier variation of beet borscht. You might even want to add some shredded cabbage to the pot. One time when too many ingredients won't spoil the cook!

TOMATO–BEEF BORSCHT

1 one-pound can tomatoes
1 bunch beets, peeled and shredded
2 quarts water
1 onion
3 neck bones
Juice of half a lemon
2 tablespoons brown sugar
1 teaspoon salt

Empty tomatoes into a large heavy saucepan. Add shredded beets, water, onion, and neck bones. Add lemon juice, brown sugar, and salt. Stir. Bring to a boil; reduce heat and simmer for 2 hours. Remove neck bones and cut up meat; return meat to the soup. Makes 8 servings.

)❭✦❭)

Do include the bay leaf in this soup. It has a pungent
seasoning flavor all its own!

1/1/81 =
Not seasoned
well enough,

BARLEY BEAN SOUP

1 cup dried lima beans
2 quarts water
3 meaty neck bones
1 onion
2 sprigs parsley
¼ cup pearl barley
1 teaspoon salt
⅛ teaspoon pepper
1 bay leaf

Soak dried lima beans for a few hours, or overnight.
Drain and add to 2 quarts of water in a heavy saucepan.
Add neck bones, onion, and parsley. Add barley, salt, pepper, and bay leaf. Bring to a boil and then turn the heat
low and simmer for about 2 hours, or until beans and meat
are tender. Remove bones and cut up chunks of meat;
return meat to the soup. Remove bay leaf and onion.
Makes 8 servings.

)❭✦❭)

Can anyone ever forget the taste of homemade lentil
soup with floating frankfurter slices? Try a bowl full of
nostalgia tonight!

LENTIL SOUP

1 cup lentils
2 quarts water

1 onion
2 cloves
3 meaty neck bones
1 scraped carrot
1 teaspoon salt
⅛ teaspoon pepper
2 frankfurters, sliced

Soak lentils for a few hours, or overnight. Drain and add
to 2 quarts of water in a heavy saucepan. Stick cloves into
onion and add to pot. Add bones, carrot, salt, and pepper.
Bring to a boil and then turn the heat low and simmer for
about 2 hours, or until lentils are soft. Force through a
food mill, after removing onion and bones. Heat again
with sliced frankfurters and serve. Makes 8 servings.

)**)

No soaking, trimming, and chopping when you start
with frozen chopped spinach for this soup. And what did
we ever do before the electric blender came along?

SPINACH SOUP

1 10-ounce package frozen chopped spinach
3 cups chicken soup
1 hot boiled potato, peeled
½ teaspoon salt
⅛ teaspoon pepper
⅛ teaspoon nutmeg

Cook spinach as directed on the package; drain. Put in
blender with 1 cup of the chicken soup and the boiled
potato. Blend until smooth. Pour remaining chicken soup
into a saucepan; add salt, pepper, and nutmeg. Stir in

blended spinach mixture. Heat and serve. Makes 6 servings.

)♦)

You'll be glad to have chicken soup in reserve when you need it for an easy meal starter like this. If you wish, serve it in mugs and let all drink this tasty brew!

TOMATO BOUILLON

1 quart tomato juice
2 cups chicken soup
1 tablespoon lemon juice
1 teaspoon sugar
½ teaspoon dillweed

Combine tomato juice with chicken soup; add lemon juice, sugar, and dillweed. Simmer for 10 minutes and serve hot. Makes 8 servings.

)♦((

4. Soup Accompaniments

))❖))))❖))))❖))))❖))))❖))))❖))))❖))))❖))))❖))))❖))))❖))))❖))))❖))))❖))))❖))))❖))))❖))❖))

In Jewish cuisine, what goes into the soup is almost as important as the soup itself. In fact, it is not unlikely to find a combination of several soup accompaniments floating in the traditional chicken soup. Here is a group of healthier recipes for old-time favorites that are especially good in chicken soup, but may lend themselves to other soups as well!

))❖))

When you make your own noodles, you cut them as thin or thick as you please. Store them in a tightly covered jar when completely dry, and they will last for several weeks.

HOMEMADE NOODLES

1 egg
2 tablespoons water
¼ teaspoon salt
½ cup flour

34

Beat egg, water, and salt together. Slowly add flour until a soft dough is formed. Roll dough out thin and let dry for about 20 minutes. Then roll dough up jelly roll fashion, and slice thin. Spread noodles out to dry. To cook, drop in boiling water or broth for 10 minutes. Serve in hot soup. Makes enough for 6 servings of soup.

:)>•>)

Not a drop of chicken fat is needed to hold these matzo balls together! Beaten egg white is the secret weapon here, so try it this healthier way.

FLUFFY MATZO BALLS

10/31/81
1/3 recipe —
VERY hard

3 eggs, separated
¾ cup matzo meal
1 tablespoon chopped parsley
½ teaspoon salt

Add dash of ginger
(½ tsp grated onion)

Beat egg yolks with a fork until lemon-colored. Stir in matzo meal, parsley, and salt. Beat egg whites separately until stiff peaks form; fold this into the egg yolk mixture. Chill. Remove from refrigerator and form into one-inch balls. Drop these in salted boiling water or broth and cook for about 20 minutes. Makes about 8 servings.

:)>•>)

Don't skip the chilling step when you prepare this recipe. It's needed to thicken and form the mixture easily into balls. Wetting your hands is a neat way to cope with forming the balls!

lee prev pg

FARINA KNAIDLACH

2 eggs, separated
1 teaspoon peanut oil
1 cup uncooked farina
1 teaspoon baking powder
½ teaspoon salt

Beat the yolks; stir in oil. Stir in farina, baking powder and salt. Beat egg whites stiff; fold into the egg yolk mixture. Chill for 1 hour. Form into one-inch balls and cook in boiling salted water for about ½ hour. Makes about 1 dozen knaidlach.

❂

What Fido doesn't know may not hurt him, as you scoop out the marrow of a large cooked soup bone! An old favorite with practiced palates.

MARROW MATZO BALLS

1 large soup bone
2 tablespoons marrow
4 tablespoons matzo meal
1 egg, beaten
1 teaspoon grated onion
½ teaspoon salt
⅛ teaspoon pepper
⅛ teaspoon nutmeg
Boiling water or broth

Simmer the soup bone in water for about 1 hour; remove marrow from bone. Mash the marrow and matzo meal together; add the egg, onion, salt, pepper, and nutmeg. Chill this mixture for at least 1 hour. Then form into

½-inch balls and drop into boiling water or broth. Cook for 10 minutes. Remove and drain. Serve in hot soup. Makes about 1 dozen balls.

:)✦:)

This is a nice way to use up the livers that accompany the chickens you use for soup. Just pop these liver balls into the soup the last ten minutes of cooking time before serving!

LIVER BALLS

2 chicken livers
1 egg
½ teaspoon salt
⅛ teaspoon pepper
¼ cup matzo meal

Broil chicken livers for several minutes until cooked. Mash them fine. Add the egg, salt, and pepper, and stir. Add matzo meal, making a mixture stiff enough to form into small balls. Drop them into chicken soup and cook for about 10 minutes. Makes about 1 dozen tiny balls.

:)✦:)

Here chicken soup instead of chicken fat is used to hold the mixture together. You can make these in advance, or in the last few minutes before serving time. A floating success either way!

MATZO EGG DROPS

1 egg
¼ cup chicken soup

¼ teaspoon salt
Dash pepper
⅓ cup matzo meal
Chicken soup

Beat egg; gradually beat in chicken soup. Add salt, pepper, and matzo meal; beat until very smooth. Heat chicken soup to a boiling point; keep it rolling while you drop rounded ¼ teaspoonfuls into the soup, one at a time. Cover soup and cook for about 3 minutes, then remove egg drops with a slotted spoon. Makes about 3 dozen egg drops, enough for 6 to 8 servings.

)⬩⬩)

Either fill with meat or kasha (buckwheat groats) and serve in hot soup for a hearty course. Do you notice the resemblance to won ton and ravioli? Just another example of the influence of international cooking!

KREPLACH

1 egg
2 tablespoons water
½ teaspoon salt
½ cup flour

Beat egg, water, and salt together. Slowly add flour, making a soft dough. Roll the dough thin and cut into 3-inch squares. Fill with Meat Filling or Kasha Filling (recipes follow). Fold dough over to make triangles, pressing edges tightly together. Then drop in boiling water or broth and cook for about 20 minutes. Remove and serve in hot soup. Makes 1 dozen Kreplach.

Meat Filling:
¼ pound ground lean beef
1 small onion, grated
¼ teaspoon salt
⅛ teaspoon pepper
Dash nutmeg

Combine ground beef, onion, salt, pepper, and nutmeg in a heavy skillet. Heat and stir so the meat doesn't stick to the pan, browning the meat as you stir. Remove from heat and use as filling for Kreplach above.

Kasha Filling:
¾ cup cooked kasha
1 small grated onion
¼ teaspoon salt
⅛ teaspoon pepper

Combine cooked kasha, onion, salt, and pepper. Use as filling for Kreplach above.

꒰꒱

Don't forget the pinch of ginger. It gives just the zing this traditional soup accompaniment needs!

FARFEL

1 cup flour
¼ teaspoon salt
⅛ teaspoon pepper
Pinch of ginger
1 egg, beaten

Combine flour, salt, pepper, and ginger. Add egg and work into a stiff dough. Roll into thin strips. Let dry on a board at room temperature for one hour. Then chop into small particles. Drop into boiling salted water or soup for about 10 minutes. Makes enough for 8 servings.

ᴅ♦ᴅ

This version of farfel is intended for Passover. But it is really too good to ignore the rest of the year!

MATZO FARFEL

2 slices matzo
¼ teaspoon salt
⅛ teaspoon pepper
Pinch of ginger
2 eggs, beaten
1 tablespoon corn oil margarine

Crush matzo into crumbs. Add salt, pepper, and ginger. Stir into beaten eggs. Heat margarine in a skillet until just melted; pour in beaten mixture and cook as for scrambled eggs. Set aside to let dry. Spoon into hot soup at serving time. Makes 8 servings.

ᴅ♦ᴅ

Add these dumplings to any of the bean, barley, or cabbage soups for a hearty course of good eating. Again, wet your hands before forming the balls and it will be simpler to do!

POTATO DUMPLINGS

2 cups grated raw potato
1 tablespoon grated onion
1 egg, beaten
¼ cup matzo meal

½ teaspoon salt
½ teaspoon dillweed

Drain grated potato in a strainer. Stir grated potato and onion into beaten egg. Add matzo meal, salt, and dillweed. Chill. Form into 1-inch balls and drop into boiling salted water; cook for about 20 minutes or until dumplings bob up to the surface. Drain and serve in hot soup. Makes 8 servings.

)▶◆)

5. Dairy Dishes

)♦:

Special care is needed to keep dairy meals both filling and in a variety of forms. This chapter has a wealth of blintzes, noodle dishes, egg creations, and casseroles to keep your meals interesting and nutritious. You will notice that only vegetable fats are used, and even those are eliminated whenever such a step seems possible. It's a healthier way to deal with dairy meals which are usually notoriously loaded with saturated fats!

)♦)

If you bake your blintzes, as directed in the recipe that follows, you will omit the second stage of frying the blintzes in oil. If you prefer to use the frying method, do remember to use an unsaturated vegetable fat!

BAKED BLINTZES

4 eggs
1 cup skim milk

1 cup flour
½ teaspoon salt
Peanut oil

Beat eggs and milk together. Slowly stir in flour and salt and beat until batter is smooth. Brush a 6-inch skillet with peanut oil. Heat and spoon in just enough batter to lightly cover the bottom of the pan. Cook until batter solidifies and is lightly browned on one side. Turn out onto a clean linen or paper towel, and continue to make the crepes one at a time, being careful to brush the skillet each time with a minimum of peanut oil to prevent sticking. When you have used up all of the batter, place 2 tablespoons of filling on the browned side of a crepe, turn up the bottom and turn in the sides. Then roll up. (At this point the blintzes may be refrigerated to cook later in the day.) Arrange blintzes in a greased baking pan and place in a 350°F. oven for 25 minutes, or until lightly browned. Serve hot. Makes about 1 dozen blintzes.

Apple Filling:
2 apples, chopped
½ cup chopped walnuts
1 tablespoon honey
¼ teaspoon cinnamon

Combine the chopped apples and walnuts. Stir in honey and cinnamon. Use as filling for blintzes.

Blueberry Filling:
1 cup blueberries
2 tablespoons sugar
2 teaspoons cornstarch
1 tablespoon grated lemon rind

Combine the blueberries and sugar; sprinkle with cornstarch and grated lemon rind and toss slightly to coat well. Use as filling for blintzes.

Cheese Filling:
1½ cups cottage cheese, drained
1 egg yolk
1 teaspoon sugar
¼ teaspoon cinnamon
½ teaspoon vanilla

Combine drained cheese with egg yolk. Stir in sugar, cinnamon, and vanilla. Use as filling for blintzes.

))✧))

This raisin-nut noodle pudding may be baked instead in a flat pan, cut in squares, and used in place of potatoes in a non-dairy meal. Or double it for a buffet offering. Or just serve it as intended with a garden salad on the side!

RAISIN–NUT NOODLE PUDDING

8 ounces broad noodles
½ cup seedless raisins
½ cup chopped nuts
¼ cup corn oil margarine
¼ cup sugar
1 egg
½ teaspoon cinnamon

Cook noodles as directed on the package, then drain and rinse; drain again. Place in a bowl and toss with raisins and nuts. Beat margarine and sugar together until fluffy; then add egg and cinnamon and beat through. Add to noodles and toss lightly until thoroughly mixed. Pour into a greased baking casserole and bake in a 350°F. oven for 45 minutes, or until browned. Makes 6 servings.

)+)

Notice how the saturated fats have been replaced with unsaturated vegetable fat and skim milk products in this recipe. But not a bit of good taste has been removed!

COTTAGE CHEESE NOODLE PUDDING

8 ounces broad noodles
¼ cup corn oil margarine
1 cup low-fat cottage cheese
1 cup plain yoghurt
2 tablespoons lemon juice
1 teaspoon vanilla
¼ cup brown sugar
½ teaspoon cinnamon
½ cup seedless raisins

Boil the noodles as directed on the package; drain and toss with bits of margarine. Stir the cottage cheese, yoghurt, lemon juice and vanilla together; add brown sugar, cinnamon, and raisins. Toss mixture lightly through the noodles. Spoon into a well-greased baking dish and bake in a 350°F. oven for 1 hour, or until lightly browned. Makes 6 servings.

)+)

There are oodles of things to do with noodles! Here is a ring mold coated with graham cracker crumbs. Unmold it carefully on a bed of parsley and slice in thick chunks!

See prev pg

GRAHAM NOODLE RING

8 ounces medium noodles
2 tablespoons corn oil margarine
1 cup crushed graham cracker crumbs
1 cup white seedless raisins

Cook noodles as directed on package. Drain. Add margarine and mix through until melted. Add ½ cup of the graham cracker crumbs and all of the raisins; mix thoroughly. Brush ring mold with corn oil and sprinkle with remaining ½ cup graham cracker crumbs. Fill with noodle mixture. Bake in a 350°F. oven for 45 minutes, or until browned. Make 6 servings. *Unmold on bed of parsley*

)❖)

Tuna fills this double layer of noodles, and tomato juice keeps everything juicy while baking. A perfect luncheon dish!

TUNA NOODLE CASSEROLE

8 ounces broad noodles
2 7-ounce cans tuna, drained
1 teaspoon celery salt
¼ teaspoon pepper
¼ teaspoon thyme
2 cups tomato juice

Cook noodles as directed on the package; drain. Flake tuna. Pour half the noodles into the bottom of a greased 2-quart casserole; top with flaked tuna, celery salt, pepper, and thyme. Cover with remaining noodles. Pour tomato juice over top. Bake in a 350°F. oven for 20 minutes or until top noodles are lightly browned. Makes 6 servings.

)I◆)I

Everybody loves macaroni! And here it is suspended in a cottage cheese-custard-like filling. A healthy and hearty dairy dish.

MACARONI–CHEESE BAKE

8 ounces elbow macaroni
4 eggs
2 cups skim milk
1½ cups creamed cottage cheese
1 teaspoon Worcestershire sauce
1 teaspoon salt
⅛ teaspoon pepper
3 tablespoons corn oil margarine
⅔ cup chopped onion
⅔ cup chopped celery
3 tablespoons chopped parsley
3 tablespoons chopped pimiento

Cook macaroni as directed on the package; drain. Beat eggs; add milk. Stir in cottage cheese, Worcestershire sauce, salt, and pepper. Stir in cooked macaroni. Melt margarine in a skillet; sauté onion and celery until limp, then add this to the macaroni mixture. Add parsley and pimiento. Pour into a greased 2-quart casserole and bake in a 350°F. oven for 1 hour. Makes 6 to 8 servings.

)I◆)I

The following is almost in the realm of soufflés and a wonderful way to serve dry cottage cheese. Do include the subtle dillweed for delicate flavor!

COTTAGE CHEESE CASSEROLE

4 eggs, separated
2 cups sieved dry or pot style cottage cheese
¼ cup mayonnaise
¼ cup yoghurt
1 teaspoon lemon juice
½ teaspoon dillweed

Beat egg whites until stiff peaks form when beater is raised. Beat egg yolks in a large bowl until light and thick; gradually add cottage cheese and stir well. Add mayonnaise, yoghurt, lemon juice and dillweed, beating until smooth. Fold egg whites into cheese mixture. Pour into a greased 1-quart casserole or soufflé dish. Bake in a 350°F. oven for 40 to 45 minutes, or until knife inserted halfway between center and edge comes out clean. Serve immediately. Makes 4 servings.

)❖)》

This version of matzo brei is done the healthier way. The skim milk and margarine lower the saturated intake of the regular version.

MATZO BREI

2 matzos
½ cup skim milk
4 eggs, beaten
¼ teaspoon salt

Dash pepper
1 tablespoon corn oil margarine

Break matzos into small pieces and place in a shallow bowl; pour milk over and stir until soft. Pour in beaten eggs, salt, and pepper; stir. Melt margarine in a skillet; pour in egg mixture. Cook over low heat until bottom of omelet is lightly browned, then turn and brown the other side. Serve at once with fruit jam, if desired. Makes 2 servings.

꜡❂꜡

Apricot jam is the surprise filling in this breakfast or luncheon omelet. Separating the eggs makes it extra fluffy!

APRICOT OMELET

4 eggs, separated
¼ teaspoon salt
1 tablespoon flour
1 tablespoon softened corn oil margarine
1 tablespoon water
2 tablespoons apricot jam

Beat egg whites with salt until stiff but not dry. Beat egg yolks with flour, softened margarine, and water. Fold the two mixtures together. Heat a lightly greased skillet and pour in mixture. Cover tightly and reduce heat; cook for about 8 minutes or until surface of omelet is solidified. Quickly spread apricot jam over surface and fold omelet in half. Makes 2 to 3 servings.

꜡❂꜡

Noodles make this omelet extra filling and extra good. The flavor of onions and celery seed combine to tickle your taste buds!

CELERY SEED NOODLE OMELET

4 ounces fine noodles
2 tablespoons chopped onion
2 tablespoons corn oil margarine
4 eggs
2 tablespoons water
½ teaspoon celery seed
½ teaspoon salt
⅛ teaspoon pepper

Cook noodles as directed on the package; drain. Cook chopped onion in margarine, using a large skillet. When onions are soft, add noodles and stir. Beat eggs, water, celery seed, salt, and pepper together; pour over noodles in the skillet. Push mixture aside as it cooks to permit uncooked portions to flow to the bottom of the pan. When mixture is completely set, fold in half and serve. Makes 2 to 3 servings.

)‡)

Even Popeye would love spinach served this way! If two eggs are against doctor's orders, cut it down to one. Either way, it's an elegant luncheon or dinner dish.

BAKED EGGS FLORENTINE

1 10-ounce package frozen spinach
8 eggs
½ teaspoon salt

⅛ teaspoon pepper
Dash nutmeg

Cook spinach as directed on the package; drain. Spoon spinach into the bottom of 4 slightly greased ramekins; break 2 eggs on top of spinach in each ramekin. Sprinkle with salt, pepper, and a bit of nutmeg. Bake in a 325°F. oven for 15 to 20 minutes, until eggs are firm. Serve in the ramekins. Makes 4 servings.

)❖)

These are simple no-nonsense scrambled eggs, fluffed up with skim milk. Follow the directions for a moist result!

FLUFFY SCRAMBLED EGGS

4 eggs
¼ cup skim milk
½ teaspoon salt
⅛ teaspoon pepper
1 tablespoon corn oil margarine
1 tablespoon chopped parsley

Beat eggs, skim milk, salt, and pepper together. Melt margarine in a large skillet; pour in egg mixture. Gently lift set edges so the uncooked portions can flow underneath. When all is thick but still moist, remove from heat and sprinkle with chopped parsley. Makes 2 servings.

)❖)

Somehow this ends up tasting like a cheese blintz, but with none of the work of making it. Be sure to leave large lumps of cottage cheese visible as you stir into the eggs!

see prev pg

SCRAMBLED COTTAGE CHEESE

4 eggs
¼ teaspoon salt
⅛ teaspoon pepper
1 tablespoon corn oil margarine
½ cup cottage cheese
1 tablespoon chopped chives
Dash paprika

Beat eggs, salt, and pepper together. Melt margarine in a skillet; pour in egg mixture. Push cooked egg to the center as uncooked egg flows to the edges to solidify. Stir cottage cheese quickly through the egg mixture the last moment of cooking. Remove from heat, sprinkle with chives, and a colorful dash of paprika. Makes 2 servings.

)‣)

6. Tasty Fish

)❖)❖

Fish is a highly recommended food for those who are watching their cholesterol level and for those who are watching their weight. Several meals of fish a week, to replace the fattier beef meals you may be used to, can be equally delicious if you take the time to use good recipes. Here are a collection of fish dishes that will have you cooking the healthier way and loving every bite!

)❖))

An electric grinder will make quick work of making gefilte fish. Wetting your hands will make it easy to handle the mixture. Once you have made it from this recipe, you will wonder why you ever relied on the jarred variety!

GEFILTE FISH

2 onions
3 carrots
3 sprigs parsley

1 quart water
1 tablespoon salt
1 tablespoon sugar
4 pounds whitefish, filleted, reserving heads, skin, and bones
2 pounds winter carp, filleted, reserving heads, skin, and bones
2 onions
3 eggs, beaten
⅓ cup matzo meal
1 tablespoon salt
½ teaspoon white pepper
Horseradish

Prepare stock base by placing 2 onions, carrots, parsley, water, 1 tablespoon salt and 1 tablespoon sugar, in a large deep kettle. Add heads, skin and bones of the fish and bring to a boil. Meanwhile, grind the fish and 2 onions together; add beaten eggs, matzo meal, salt, pepper, and sugar. If mixture seems too thick, add several tablespoons of ice water. Wet hands and form oval balls (about ⅓ cup of the mixture for each ball); then drop them carefully into the simmering stock. Cover and cook for 2 hours, then remove fish balls and boil the stock to reduce it in volume. Strain stock. Cut carrots into slices. Refrigerate gefilte fish covered with stock and carrots, so the stock will jell. Serve with some of the jellied stock, several carrot slices on each piece of fish, and pass the horseradish. Makes about 16 pieces of fish.

)▶✧◀)

Baked gefilte fish tastes a little drier than the boiled variety of the previous recipe, but is faster to make. Worth doing when smaller amounts of fish are desired!

BAKED GEFILTE FISH PATTIES

3 pounds halibut or pike
2 eggs
½ cup water
½ teaspoon salt
¼ teaspoon pepper
3 tablespoons matzo meal
2 onions, chopped fine
1 tablespoon margarine

Skin, fillet and grind the fish, or have it done for you at the fishmarket. Beat eggs and water together; add salt and pepper. Add egg mixture to the fish alternately with the matzo meal. Sauté the onions in margarine until they are tender and translucent; add to the fish mixture. Form the fish into large thick patties and place in a large baking dish. When all are in place, cover them with water. Bake at 350°F. for about 1 hour. Water will evaporate and fish patties will be lightly browned. Makes about 10 patties.

When the batter has zest, the end result will be tasty too. Here is a healthier way to cook breaded fish than the usual frying method, and what could be faster to do!

BROILED SPICY FISH FILLETS

6 fillets of flounder or haddock
1 egg
1 teaspoon prepared mustard
2 tablespoons lemon juice
1 teaspoon Worcestershire sauce
½ teaspoon salt

½ teaspoon paprika
½ cup matzo meal
1 tablespoon corn oil margarine

Wash and wipe fish fillets. Beat egg and stir in mustard, lemon juice, Worcestershire sauce, salt, and paprika. Dip fish fillets in the egg mxiture and then into matzo meal. Arrange on a broiling pan. Dot with margarine. Broil until fish flakes and crumbs are browned, about 15 minutes. Makes 6 servings.

)❖)

This flounder wears its own topping right to the table. Again, the Italian influence at work in Jewish cuisine!

BROILED FLOUNDER PARMESAN

1 pound fillets of flounder
½ teaspoon salt
⅛ teaspoon pepper
2 tomatoes, skinned and chopped
1 tablespoon grated onion
½ teaspoon oregano
2 tablespoons grated Parmesan cheese

Arrange flounder fillets on a broiling pan. Season with salt and pepper. Spoon chopped tomatoes over the fillets; add grated onion, oregano, and then grated cheese. Broil for 10 to 15 minutes, or until fish flakes easily. Makes 4 servings.

)❖)

Long a favorite of old-time cooks, this boiled fish is juicy and nutritious. The bay leaf and cloves give a slightly pungent flavor!

BOILED FISH

4 one-pound cod or halibut steaks
1 small onion, diced
1 carrot, peeled and diced
1 sprig parsley
2 quarts water
½ cup tarragon vinegar
2 teaspoons salt
1 teaspoon sugar
1 bay leaf
2 whole cloves

Arrange fish steaks in the bottom of a heavy saucepan, preferably on a rack. Add onion, carrot, and parsley. Cover with water and vinegar; add salt, sugar, bay leaf, and cloves. Bring quickly to the boiling point; lower heat to keep liquid just below the boiling point. Cook for 10 to 15 minutes, or just until fish flakes easily. Makes 4 servings.

:)◆:)

Serve this boiled carp with the herb dressing on page 64 for a wonderful dining experience. Don't overcook fish if you want to enjoy it at its best!

BOILED CARP

4 slices fresh carp
1 onion, sliced thin

1 teaspoon salt
½ teaspoon sugar
2 peppercorns
1 bay leaf
Boiling water

Arrange fish slices in the bottom of a heavy saucepan. Add onion slices, salt, sugar, peppercorns and bay leaf. Cover with boiling water. Cover pan and simmer for 30 minutes, or until fish flakes easily. Makes 4 servings.

)❖)

This sauce is quick to prepare and pour over the fish for baking. Produces a dish that's sure to please!

BAKED HADDOCK FILLETS

2 pounds haddock fillets
1 8-ounce can tomato sauce
1 small onion, diced
1 clove garlic, minced
1 small green pepper, diced
2 tablespoons lemon juice
1 teaspoon Worcestershire sauce
1 teaspoon sugar
½ teaspoon salt
¼ teaspoon pepper

Arrange haddock fillets in a greased baking dish. Combine remaining ingredients in a small saucepan; simmer for 5 minutes. Pour sauce over fillets. Bake in a 350°F. oven for 20 minutes, or until fish flakes easily. Makes 6 servings.

)❖)

The dish pictured on the jacket is as intriguing in taste as it is in appearance. A blend of Danish cheese and mushrooms gives a fine flavor!

SOLE ROLLS

4 medium fillets of sole
1 3½-ounce Buko (cheese with mushroom) cup
1 sliced tomato
½ cup white wine
½ teaspoon salt
⅛ teaspoon pepper
2 tablespoons corn oil margarine

Spread one side of each fillet with cheese mixture; roll up. Arrange fillets in a greased ovenproof dish, add a layer of tomato slices and pour wine over fish. Sprinkle with salt and pepper. Dot the top with margarine. Cover dish and cook on top of the stove over low heat for 15–20 minutes or until fillets are tender. Makes 4 servings.

꒦꒦

For the squeamish, have your fishman cut off the head and tail. The rest is cut into large chunks at serving time, and then perhaps garnished with lemon and parsley. The stuffing can replace a potato for those who are calorie counting!

STUFFED BAKED BLUEFISH

1 whole bluefish, about 4 pounds, cleaned
2 tablespoons corn oil margarine
1 small onion, diced

1 cup matzo meal
1 teaspoon finely chopped parsley
1 tablespoon chopped dill pickle
½ teaspoon salt
¼ cup skim milk
1 lemon

Melt margarine in a skillet; saute onion until tender. Stir into matzo meal; add parsley, pickle, and salt. Stir in milk. Wash and wipe bluefish; stuff with prepared mixture. Cut lemon in half and squeeze juice over fish. Place fish in a greased pan. Bake for 15 minutes per pound of fish in a 375°F. oven. Makes 4 servings.

)❖)❮

For a non-dairy meal, eleminate the yoghurt and replace it with an additional ½ cup tomato sauce. Either way, it is a delectable dish!

HALIBUT LOAF

2 pounds halibut, cooked, boned and flaked
1 chopped green pepper
1 chopped onion
2 stalks chopped celery
½ cup mayonnaise
½ cup yoghurt
2 teaspoons Worcestershire sauce
1 8-ounce can tomato sauce

Combine flaked halibut, green pepper, onion, and celery. Combine mayonnaise, yoghurt, and Worcestershire sauce; stir through fish mixture. Turn into a greased loaf pan. Pour tomato sauce over top. Bake in 425°F. oven for 20 minutes. Makes 6 servings.

)•◊•)

This salad is perfect for a light summer meal. If serving to guests, pack it first into a shaped mold and then turn upside down on a bed of lettuce—much like making mud pies so long ago!

HALIBUT SALAD

1 medium onion, sliced
1 lemon slice
1 bay leaf
½ teaspoon salt
2 cups water
2 pounds halibut steaks
3 hard-cooked eggs, chopped
1½ cups diced celery
⅓ cup mayonnaise
⅓ cup yoghurt
½ cup chili sauce
1 tablespoon lemon juice
Lettuce cups

Add onion, lemon slice, bay leaf and salt to water in a large skillet over medium heat. Bring to a boil. Add fish in a single layer. Cover; reduce heat and simmer for 5 minutes or until fish flakes easily with a fork. Remove fish and cool. Flake fish, discarding skin and bones. Mix together egg, celery, mayonnaise, yoghurt, chili sauce and lemon juice. Add flaked fish and toss until thoroughly mixed. Chill. Makes 8 servings.

)•◊•)

Do prepare the cucumber sauce that should accompany this salmon dish. It adds the tender touch of color and flavor!

BOILED SALMON WITH CUCUMBER SAUCE

4 small salmon steaks
Boiling water
{ 1 lemon, sliced thin
{ ½ teaspoon salt
1 cup plain yoghurt
{ 1 cucumber, chopped
{ 2 tablespoons chopped chives
{ 1 tablespoon lemon juice
{ ½ teaspoon salt
{ ½ teaspoon minced fresh dill

Place salmon steaks on a rack in the bottom of a fish poacher or large skillet. Cover with boiling water. Add sliced lemon and salt. Simmer for about 10 minutes, or until fish flakes easily but holds its shape. Remove fish and serve hot or cold with Cucumber Sauce. Makes 4 servings.

Cucumber Sauce:
Empty yoghurt into a bowl. Stir in chopped cucumber and chives. Add lemon juice, salt, and dill. Add green food coloring, if desired. Makes 1¼ cups of sauce.

꩜

Here's a good recipe to have when you need an economy meal or you forgot to market. Everything needed is probably in your kitchen right now!

Good 6/3/81. Used 2 c cooked rice in place of potatoes. A little fishy.

BAKED SALMON LOAF

1 16-ounce can red salmon, drained and cleaned
1 chopped onion
1 chopped green pepper
2 medium-sized potatoes, cooked, peeled and shredded
1 egg, slightly beaten
1 tablespoon mayonnaise
1 teaspoon prepared mustard
½ teaspoon salt
⅛ teaspoon pepper   *Try dill weed.*

Flake salmon and add onion, green pepper, and shredded potatoes. Combine egg, mayonnaise, mustard, salt, and pepper. Mix through salmon mixture. Turn into a greased loaf pan, pressing down evenly. Bake in 375°F. oven for 25 minutes. Makes 4 to 6 servings.

)❋)

Pickled Salmon is one of the favorites of Jewish cuisine. No need to buy at the deli—make it yourself with the recipe that follows!

PICKLED SALMON

2 pounds fresh salmon, sliced
2 onions, sliced thin
2 teaspoons salt
1 teaspoon whole mixed spices
⅛ teaspoon pepper
½ cup sugar
¾ cup wine vinegar
½ cup water

Place salmon slices in the bottom of a small casserole that has a tight-fitting lid. Cover with onion slices. Stir salt, whole mixed spices, pepper, and sugar into the wine vinegar. Add water and stir briskly; pour the mixture over the salmon. Refrigerate covered, for several hours or overnight. Then simmer for 25 minutes. Cool and chill. To serve, cut salmon slices into bite-sized pieces.

)❯)

If you are used to eating baked herring, try this way of removing the skin with ease. If you're not used to this dish, take a taste!

BAKED HERRING

2 large whole miltz herrings
Boiling water
2 teaspoons corn oil

Arrange cleaned herrings in a flat pan and cover with boiling water. Let stand about 20 minutes. Then drain and remove skin. Brush with corn oil and bake in a 350°F. oven for 15 minutes. Serve hot. Makes 4 servings.

)❯)

Many fish dishes almost beg for a dressing. Here's an easy way to concoct a toothsome topping!

HERB DRESSING FOR SEAFOOD

½ cup mayonnaise
½ cup yoghurt
1 tablespoon finely chopped parsley

1½ teaspoons chopped chives
1½ teaspoons dried tarragon leaves
½ teaspoon chopped dill or dried dillweed

Mix together the mayonnaise and yoghurt. Add the parsley, chives, tarragon, and dill. Chill at least 2 hours before serving. Makes 1 cup of dressing.

)❖)

Prefer a spicy tomato-based sauce? This one's good for dipping too. Easy on the horseradish if you're not used to it!

COCKTAIL SAUCE FOR FISH

½ cup catsup
½ cup chili sauce
1 tablespoon sweet pickle relish
1 tablespoon white horseradish
1 teaspoon Worcestershire sauce

Stir the catsup and chili sauce together. Add the relish, horseradish, and Worcestershire sauce. Chill to let mixture blend for several hours before serving. Makes about 1 cup, or enough for 6 servings of fish.

)❖)

7. Delicious Poultry

))+:

If you learn to eat the healthier way, there will be many poultry meals on your table. But the versatility that is possible with poultry will keep your family content to see it again and again in different forms. Whenever possible, skim the fat out of the sauce to reduce the intake of saturated fat. And don't be chicken when it comes to trying many of these new dishes!

))+))

Pop some peeled potatoes and raw vegetables into the pot during the last half-hour of cooking, and you will have a one-pot meal that can't be beat!

POTTED CHICKEN

1 3-pound chicken, cut up
¾ teaspoon salt
¼ teaspoon pepper
1 one-pound can tomatoes

1 onion, sliced thin
½ cup dry white wine
1 tablespoon lemon juice
¼ teaspoon thyme
1 teaspoon sugar

Place chicken in a heavy saucepan. Season with salt and pepper. Add tomatoes, onion, wine, and lemon juice. Add thyme and sugar. Cover and cook over low heat for 45 minutes, or until chicken is tender. Makes 4 servings.

)❉)

Tiny split broilers are a good meal for those times when you are in a hurry. These will be especially delicious with their herb coating!

1/11/81—Not great; herb coating made little difference.

HERB BROILED CHICKEN

2 small split broiler chickens, about 2 pounds each
1 tablespoon vegetable oil
2 tablespoons lemon juice
¼ teaspoon salt
⅛ teaspoon pepper
⅛ teaspoon rosemary

Place halves of chicken on a broiling pan, skin side down. Combine oil, lemon juice, salt, pepper, and rosemary, stirring well. Brush half of this mixture on top of chicken and broil for 10 minutes. Turn chicken, brush the skin side with the remaining mixture and broil for 10 minutes more, or until tender. Makes 4 servings.

)❉)

This is the way to have baked chicken! Succulent sauce moistens and smothers the bird into tenderness. Plan for seconds on this one.

BARBECUED CHICKEN

2 broiler chickens, cut in parts
½ cup chili sauce
¼ cup water
¼ cup wine vinegar
2 tablespoons olive oil
2 teaspoons Worcestershire sauce
½ teaspoon dry mustard
½ teaspoon salt
⅛ teaspoon pepper

Arrange chicken parts in a large baking pan. Combine remaining ingredients in a saucepan; stir and heat for 5 minutes. Then pour the barbecue sauce over the chicken and bake in a 350°F. oven for 45 to 55 minutes, or until chicken is tender. Baste occasionally. Makes 8 servings.

)⬧)‑

Did you know that lemon and chicken have a thing for each other? True. And here with fresh dill it emerges rich with flavor.

LEMON DILL CHICKEN

2 broiler chickens, cut in parts
3 tablespoons corn oil
⅓ cup lemon juice
1 tablespoon chopped fresh dill

½ teaspoon salt
½ teaspoon paprika

Arrange chicken in a flat baking dish. Combine the oil, lemon juice, dill, salt, and paprika; pour over chicken parts. Cover with foil or a tight fitting lid and bake in a 350°F. oven for 45 minutes, or until tender. Uncover the baking dish the last 10 minutes so chicken will brown. Makes 8 servings.

)◆)

There's a bit of Chinese influence in the ingredients for this chicken dish, and the results are very enjoyable. The bit of ginger makes you savor every morsel!

SWEET AND SOUR CHICKEN

2 broiler chickens, cut in parts
½ cup brown sugar
½ cup water
¼ cup soy sauce
2 tablespoons corn oil
¼ cup pineapple juice
½ teaspoon garlic powder
½ teaspoon ground ginger

Place chicken parts in a large plastic bag, set into a deep bowl. Combine sugar, water, soy sauce, corn oil, pineapple juice, garlic powder, and ginger. Pour this mixture over the chicken and fasten the bag closed. Place in refrigerator for at least 3 hours, turning the bag occasionally to redistribute the marinade. When ready to cook, place chicken parts in a flat baking pan and pour the remaining marinade over all. Bake in a 350°F. oven for 1 hour, or until tender. Makes 8 servings.

)❖)

No need to fry chicken ever again! Now you can bake it crispy and mouth-watering good.

BAKED CRISP CHICKEN

1 3-pound frying chicken, cut up
1 cup corn flake crumbs
¼ teaspoon crushed oregano
¼ teaspoon garlic salt
½ teaspoon paprika
½ teaspoon salt
¼ cup corn oil

Wash and dry chicken pieces. Combine corn flake crumbs, oregano, garlic salt, paprika, and salt. Brush skin of chicken parts with corn oil, then coat each piece with corn flake mixture. Place skin side up in a single layer in a foil-lined pan. Bake in a 350°F. oven for about 1 hour or until tender. Makes 4 servings.

)❖)

A salad is all you'll need to complete this meal-in-one. Add a drop of olive oil to the water when spaghetti is cooking, to prevent strands from sticking together.

CHICKEN IN SPAGHETTI SAUCE

1 tablespoon olive oil
2 onions, diced
1 clove garlic, minced
2 broiler chickens, cut up

2 16-ounce cans tomatoes packed in tomato puree
1 8-ounce can tomato sauce
1 teaspoon salt
¼ teaspoon pepper
¼ teaspoon basil
2 green peppers, diced
¼ pound fresh mushrooms, sliced
1 tablespoon salt
4 quarts boiling water
1 one-pound package spaghetti

Heat olive oil in the bottom of a heavy saucepan; sauté onions and garlic for a few moments. Then add chicken pieces and brown on all sides, being careful to keep moving the chicken around so it doesn't scorch. Add tomatoes, tomato sauce, salt, pepper, and basil. Cover saucepan tightly and simmer for 30 minutes. Add green pepper and mushrooms and simmer 10 minutes more. During last 15 minutes of cooking, prepare spaghetti by adding salt to rapidly boiling water and gradually adding spaghetti so that water continues to boil. Cook uncovered, stirring occasionally, until tender. Drain in colander. Serve topped with chicken and sauce. Makes 8 servings.

)**⟩

It's a whole meal in a skillet this time, and you can prepare it from start to finish in a cool twenty minutes. Keep it in mind next time you're in a hurry!

6/19/80 Very good. ↳

CHICKEN SKILLET

3 whole broiler-fryer chicken breasts
¼ cup corn oil margarine

2 teaspoons salt
1 teaspoon monosodium glutamate
2 teaspoons parsley flakes
1 teaspoon leaf thyme
1 10-ounce package frozen peas
1 cup diagonally-sliced celery
1 medium onion, sliced
1 cup chicken soup
1 20½-ounce can pineapple chunks w̄ syrup
2 tablespoons cornstarch
¼ cup cold water
1 tablespoon Worcestershire sauce
1 tomato, peeled and cut into 6 wedges
Hot cooked rice

Used ½ of syrup; ½ of that amt. of sherry; 1 c. chicken soup

added last

Bone chicken breasts; remove skin; cut chicken in strips, about 10 to each breast half. Melt margarine in large skillet over high heat; add chicken and sprinkle with salt, monosodium glutamate, parsley and thyme. Cook, stirring constantly, for 3 minutes. Add peas; break up with fork. Add celery and onion; continue stirring and cooking 2 minutes. Add chicken soup and pineapple with syrup. Bring to a boil; reduce heat to medium and cook, covered, 4 minutes. Blend together cornstarch, water and Worcestershire sauce. Stir all at once into skillet. Cook over high heat, stirring rapidly, until thickened. Add tomatoes. Serve over hot cooked rice. Makes 6 servings.

)•)

You'll really have a way with chopped chicken livers when you learn to make this sauce. It's extra nutritious too!

SPAGHETTI WITH CHICKEN LIVER SAUCE

1 cup bouillon
1 onion, chopped fine
½ pound chicken livers, chopped
¼ pound fresh mushrooms, sliced
1 teaspoon salt
¼ teaspoon pepper
¼ teaspoon thyme
1 8-ounce can tomato sauce
1 tablespoon flour
12 ounces spaghetti
4 quarts boiling water

Pour bouillon into a large skillet; add chopped onion, livers, and mushrooms. Cook over moderate heat for 5 minutes, stirring occasionally. Add salt, pepper and thyme, and mix through. Combine tomato sauce and flour; stir into liver mixture. Cook for 8 to 10 minutes over low heat, stirring until thickened. Meanwhile, drop spaghetti into boiling water and cook for 12 minutes, or until al dente. Drain, and serve with sauce. Makes 4 servings.

꒰꒱

This recipe can be used as an appetizer, served on toast points, or as a main course served on hot rice. Either way, you'll like it!

CHICKEN LIVERS WITH ONIONS

½ cup chicken broth
2 onions, sliced thin
1½ pounds chicken livers

½ pound fresh mushrooms, sliced
2 tablespoons minced parsley
1 teaspoon paprika
½ teaspoon salt
⅛ teaspoon pepper

Pour chicken broth into a large skillet. Heat and add sliced onions; cook until translucent. Add chicken livers and mushrooms; sprinkle with parsley, paprika, salt, and pepper. Cover and simmer for 10 minutes, or until livers are tender. Serve on hot cooked rice, or on toast points. Makes 4 servings.

)I✛:)

This is the chicken's answer to gefilte fish! It's made with a similar technique but makes a delicious gravy as well.

CHOPPED CHICKEN BALLS

2 whole chicken breasts (from broilers)
1 onion
1 egg
1 slice day-old bread
1 tablespoon minced fresh parsley
½ teaspoon salt
⅛ teaspoon pepper
2 cups water
2 onions, sliced thin
1 carrot, scraped and sliced thin
½ teaspoon salt
½ teaspoon sugar

Remove bones and skin from raw chicken breasts; grind in food chopper. Add one onion through grinder. Stir in egg. Soak bread with as much water as it will hold, then shred it into the mixture. Add parsley, salt, and pepper. Pour 2 cups of water into a saucepan; add sliced onions, carrots, salt, and sugar. Bring water to a boil. Form 2-inch balls of chicken mixture and gently lower into boiling water. Turn heat down to keep water just under the boiling point. Cover and cook for 35 minutes, adding more water if necessary. Serve with rice or noodles, using the gravy to ladle over all. Makes 6 servings.

)❖)

This recipe was made for Friday night dinner. But even Mama never made it so good!

ROAST CHICKEN

1 roasting chicken, about 5 pounds
1 lemon
1 teaspoon salt
½ teaspoon paprika
1 small onion, sliced
1 cup water

Arrange roasting chicken in an open pan, after cleaning and washing thoroughly. Cut lemon in half and squeeze the juice over the surfaces of the chicken, including interior. Sprinkle salt both inside and out. Sprinkle the skin with paprika. Tuck remaining squeezed-out lemon halves into the chicken. Place onion slices around the base of the chicken and pour water into the pan. Roast in a 350°F. oven about 2½ hours, basting occasionally with pan juices. Remove lemon rinds from chicken cavity before serving. Makes 4 to 6 servings.

)❖)

Don't forget to pierce the duck at high heat to let the fat run off. If you do it right, there'll be no layer of fat left under the skin at serving time!

CRISP ROAST DUCK

1 duck, about 5 pounds
1 orange
1 teaspoon salt
¼ teaspoon garlic salt

Arrange duck on a rack in an open roasting pan, after cleaning and washing thoroughly. Cut orange in half; squeeze generously over skin of duck and then tuck the remaining orange rind into the cavity of the duck. Sprinkle duck with salt and garlic salt. Roast in a 300°F. oven for 2 hours, and then turn heat up to 500° F. for 15 minutes. Pierce the skin of duck all over with a fork as it roasts to permit the layer of fat under the skin to run off; the high heat at the end of the roasting will insure the melting of any remaining fat, and the final crisping of the duck. Makes 4 servings.

꩜

The Israeli Sabra liqueur used on this turkey has a flavor of chocolate and orange. It will glaze the turkey and give it a delectable flavor!

ROAST TURKEY

1 turkey, 12 to 16 pounds
1 teaspoon salt
1 teaspoon paprika

{ ½ cup Sabra liqueur
{ 1 cup orange juice

Arrange turkey in an open roasting pan, after cleaning and washing thoroughly. Sprinkle with salt and paprika. Combine liqueur and orange juice. Pour ⅓ of the mixture over the turkey. Roast in a 300°F. oven, 20 minutes to the pound, basting frequently with the remaining orange mixture. Towards the end of roasting time, baste with pan drippings. Makes 8 to 12 servings.

꒒꒷꒒

8. *Kosher Meats*

◗◆

Only the forequarters of approved beef, lamb, and veal may be used in traditional Jewish cuisine. These limitations will have no effect on your ability to cook up a variety of savory meals. Do cut as much fat away as possible, both before and after cooking, to eliminate the most guilty possessor of saturated fats. Because of this high saturated fat content, exceptional care has been taken to present you with recipes that are unsaturated in every other way.

◗◆◗

This is simple peasant cooking at its best. Follow the lead and serve with cabbage, potatoes, or other earthy vegetables.

BOILED BEEF

1 4-pound piece beef flanken
1 onion, sliced
2 cups boiling water

1 bay leaf
½ teaspoon salt
¼ teaspoon pepper
2 sprigs fresh dill

Arrange meat in a Dutch oven. Add sliced onion and pour boiling water over all. Add bay leaf, salt, pepper, and sprigs of dill. Cover pot and simmer on top of range for about 2½ to 3 hours, or until tender. Slice and serve with fresh horseradish. Makes 8 servings.

)❖)

Trim off the excess fat and then make diagonal slashes around the edges to prevent the steak from curling up. Spread with mustard for a piquant flavor!

BROILED RIB STEAKS

4 rib steaks, about ¾ inch thick
1 teaspoon prepared mustard
½ teaspoon onion salt

Arrange rib steaks on a broiling pan. Spread with a thin coating of mustard and a sprinkling of onion salt. Broil for 7 minutes, then turn and broil for an additional 7 minutes, or longer to achieve desired degree of doneness. Makes 4 to 6 servings.

)❖)

This pot roast can be cooked entirely on top of the range, but putting it in the oven for the last part of cooking is the French way of doing it. A bit different when the heat hits from all sides!

See prev page.

POT ROAST

⅓ cup corn oil
3 pounds beef pot roast
2 onions, sliced thin
3 stalks celery, sliced thin
1 clove garlic, minced
2 cups bouillon
1 8-ounce can tomato sauce
½ teaspoon salt
¼ teaspoon pepper
¼ teaspoon basil

Heat oil in the bottom of a Dutch oven. Sear beef roast on all sides in the hot oil. Turn heat low and add sliced onions, celery, and minced garlic. Stir these around for a few minutes until they are limp. Add bouillon, tomato sauce, salt, pepper, and basil. Bring to a boil; then cover and remove from top of range and put into a 350°F. oven. Cook for 2½ to 3 hours, or until tender. Makes 8 servings.

)❂)

Add a green vegetable or a salad and once again, you have a marvelous meal-in-one. Brisket should be well-done and slow cooked for best results!

BRISKET POT ROAST

4 pounds brisket of beef
½ teaspoon salt
¼ teaspoon pepper
½ teaspoon paprika
2 onions, sliced thin
1 28-ounce can tomatoes in puree

2 bay leaves
4 scraped carrots, sliced thin
4 potatoes, peeled and quartered

Place brisket in a Dutch oven; season with salt, pepper, and paprika. Cover with sliced onions. Pour tomatoes around the brisket. Add bay leaves and sliced carrots. Cover and bake in a 325°F. oven for 2 hours. Add potatoes and continue baking, covered, for an additional 30 minutes to 1 hour, until brisket and potatoes are tender. Remove bay leaves. Slice brisket and serve with potatoes and gravy. Makes 8 to 10 servings.

꩜

For those who enjoy a more zesty flavor, this brisket with barbecue sauce is lip-smacking good. Keep the oven low and the cooking long to captivate best texture.

BRISKET WITH BARBECUE SAUCE

4 pounds brisket of beef, well trimmed
1 8-ounce can tomato sauce
½ cup water
¼ cup catsup
2 tablespoons lemon juice
2 tablespoons wine vinegar
1 tablespoon Worcestershire sauce
2 tablespoons brown sugar
½ teaspoon dry mustard
¼ teaspoon paprika
2 onions, sliced thin
1 clove garlic, minced

Arrange brisket in a Dutch oven. Combine tomato sauce, water, catsup, lemon juice, wine vinegar, and

Worcestershire sauce; stir well. Stir in brown sugar, mustard, and paprika. Pour mixture over the brisket. Top with sliced onions and minced garlic. Cover and bake in a 325°F. oven for 2½ to 3 hours, or until tender. Slice and serve with barbecue sauce. Makes 8 to 10 servings.

꒰꒱

Certainly, this can be cooked on top of the range—just simmer over low heat and add more water if needed. Either way, it's a feast indeed!

1/28/81

BAKED BEEF STEW

2 pounds boned beef cubes
1 cup Burgundy wine
½ teaspoon salt
½ teaspoon garlic powder
½ teaspoon thyme
2 bay leaves
2 tablespoons tomato paste
1 cup water
2 onions, sliced thin
6 carrots, scraped and cut in chunks
6 potatoes, scraped and cut in chunks
1 10-ounce package frozen peas

Place beef cubes in the bottom of a Dutch oven. Pour wine over meat and season with salt, garlic powder, and thyme; stir all of this and set aside for at least a half hour so wine can tenderize meat. Then add bay leaves. Stir tomato paste and water together and add, mixing all well. Add sliced onions and stir. Cover and bake in a 325°F. oven for 1½ to 2 hours. Add carrots and potatoes and bake for 20 minutes more; then add peas, stir through, and bake for 15 minutes or until vegetables are tender. Makes 6 servings.

⁂

Making a tsimmes means to make a fuss over, but the captivating aroma that fills the kitchen makes it all worthwhile. Creates a lot of hunger pangs too!

BEEF TSIMMES

4 pounds short ribs of beef
2 onions, chopped
1 clove garlic, minced
¾ teaspoon salt
¼ teaspoon pepper
½ teaspoon paprika
¼ teaspoon ginger
Boiling water
6 sweet potatoes, peeled and quartered
1 12-ounce package pitted prunes
½ cup brown sugar
1 tablespoon lemon juice

With a sharp knife, trim ribs of excess fat. Then place them on a broiler and brown on all sides, reducing fat content further. Place browned ribs in a large heavy pot and add onions and garlic. Add salt, pepper, paprika and ginger, and cover meat with boiling water. Cover pan and simmer for 1 hour. Add sweet potatoes, prunes, brown sugar, and lemon juice; cover pan again and simmer for about 40 minutes more, or until meat and sweet potatoes are completely tender. Makes 6 to 8 servings.

⁂

Once again the ingredients for this dish seem to have a Chinese influence. It's another quickie meal that's sure to please!

PEPPER STEAK

1 pound beef steak
¼ cup corn oil
½ cup diced onion
4 sweet green peppers, seeded and cut up
1 clove garlic, minced
½ teaspoon salt
¼ teaspoon pepper
¼ teaspoon ground ginger
1 tablespoon cornstarch
1 cup beef bouillon
1 tablespoon soy sauce
2 cups hot cooked rice

Cut steak diagonally across the grain into thin slices, and then cut the strips into 2-inch pieces. Heat oil in a skillet; add meat and quickly brown it on all sides. Add onion, green pepper, garlic, salt, pepper, and ginger. Cook over medium heat, stirring constantly for several minutes, until peppers are tender. Stir the cornstarch into the bouillon and then add soy sauce, making a smooth mixture. Stir this into the meat mixture and bring to a boil. Stir constantly while mixture bubbles for a minute or two; it will thicken and then clear. Serve over hot cooked rice. Makes 4 servings.

))·((

The sliced orange gives this corned beef and cabbage a flavorsome kick. Pop some peeled potatoes in if you wish to have a meal-in-one—add when you put in the cabbage wedges!

CORNED BEEF AND CABBAGE GOURMET

4 pounds corned beef (without seasonings)
Water to cover
2 cups Sauterne wine
2 stalks celery
1 small orange, sliced
1 onion, finely chopped
1 garlic clove, minced
2 bay leaves
1 teaspoon dillweed
1 teaspoon cinnamon
Dash of cayenne
1 large head of cabbage, cut in wedges

Place corned beef in a heavy saucepan or Dutch oven and cover with water. Add Sauterne, celery, orange, onion, garlic, bay leaf, dillweed, cinnamon, and cayenne. Cook together for 40 minutes to the pound. The last half hour of cooking, add cabbage wedges. Makes 6 to 8 servings.

꙰꙰

Here's what to do with corned beef left over from the previous recipe. It's a New England styled dish, known as Red Flannel Hash!

CORNED BEEF HASH

2 cups corned beef, chopped coarsely
2 cups chopped potatoes
1 cup chopped beets

1 small chopped onion
1 teaspoon salt
¼ cup water

Combine chopped corned beef, potatoes, beets, and
onion. Add salt and water. Grease a large frying pan with
corn oil, heat, then spread hash mixture evenly in the pan.
Cover and cook over low heat for 1 hour. Fold, turn, and
serve. Makes 4 servings.

ﾟﾟﾟ

This recipe is for a classic dish in Jewish cuisine. It
takes a bit of preparation time, but will win you applause
with every bite!

STUFFED CABBAGE

*1/17/81   X
Quite good —*

1 large head of cabbage
1 pound ground beef
¼ cup white rice
1 small onion, grated
1 egg, beaten
2 tablespoons water
¾ teaspoon salt
¼ teaspoon pepper
1 2-pound can tomatoes
1 lemon
⅓ cup brown sugar
1 teaspoon salt
¼ teaspoon pepper
¼ teaspoon ground ginger

Parboil the cabbage just until you can remove the outer
leaves easily. Discard the toughest outer leaves, and trim

*OR:
Separate cabbage leaves. Wash and boil them uncovered for 5 min.
in a quantity of boiling water. Reserve the liquor.*

the heavy center membrane of the remaining leaves. Combine the beef, rice, and onion. Stir the egg and water together and add to beef mixture. Add ¾ teaspoon salt and ¼ teaspoon pepper. Place a small amount of meat at the trimmed membrane end of the cabbage leaf; roll forward once, fold the sides inwards, and roll up to the top of the leaf. Repeat this until the meat mixture is used up. Cut up remaining cabbage and place in the bottom of a heavy saucepan or Dutch oven. Add tomatoes, the juice of the lemon, brown sugar, and the remaining salt, pepper, and ginger. Stir it around well. Arrange layers of stuffed cabbage rolls with the seam side down, on top of the tomato mixture. Bring to a boil on top of the range, and then cover and turn the heat low. Cook for about 2 hours, or until meat is tender. Makes 6 servings.

ᗡᗡᗡ

This meatloaf has a healthy filling of quaker oats to expand the meat and make it fluffy. Tomato juice is the flavorsome liquid used to moisten the meat.

MEATLOAF

1½ pounds ground beef
¾ cup uncooked quaker oats
1 egg, beaten
1 small onion, chopped
¾ teaspoon salt
¼ teaspoon pepper
¼ teaspoon garlic powder
1 cup tomato juice

Mix ground beef, cereal, egg, and onion together. Add salt, pepper, and garlic powder. Work in tomato juice until all is mixed well. Pack into a loaf pan and bake in a 350°F. oven for 1 hour. Makes 4 to 6 servings.

⟩⟨⟨⟩

If you're craving for a spicy slice of meatloaf, this recipe is sure to please. Goes together in minutes, and emerges from the oven with exquisite bouquet just one short hour later!

SPICY MEATLOAF

1½ pounds ground beef
½ cup water
1 egg, beaten
½ cup fine bread crumbs
1 small onion, grated
½ teaspoon salt
½ teaspoon sage
¼ teaspoon catsup
1 tablespoon brown sugar
1 teaspoon prepared mustard
¼ teaspoon nutmeg

Combine the ground beef with water and beaten egg. Add bread crumbs, grated onion, salt and sage. Pack into a loaf pan. Combine catsup, brown sugar, mustard, and nutmeg; pour over the top of the meat loaf. Bake in a 350°F. oven for 1 hour. Makes 4 to 6 servings.

⟩⟨⟨⟩

Want savory meatballs for a pick-me-up appetizer? Try these meatballs in plum sauce for a taste that's different and oh-so-good!

MEATBALLS IN PLUM SAUCE

1½ pounds lean ground beef
1 one-pound can purple plums
2 tablespoons red wine vinegar
⅔ cup tomato catsup
1½ teaspoons candied ginger, finely minced
1 teaspoon salt
½ teaspoon chili powder
¼ teaspoon garlic powder
1 small onion, minced

Form ground beef into tiny meatballs and place in a heavy saucepan. Remove pits and put plums and syrup into an electric blender; puree. Add enough water to the pureed plums to make 2½ cups. Add vinegar, catsup, ginger, salt, chili powder, garlic powder, and onion. Pour sauce over the meatballs and simmer slowly for about 30 minutes. Serve on picks as an appetizer or as a main course. Makes 6 servings.

〉〉✦〉〉

When you think of sauerbraten, think of red cabbage, potato pancakes, and seasoning of ginger. It's a combination to stimulate the weakest appetite!

SAUERBRATEN MEATBALLS

1½ pounds ground beef
1 onion, grated
½ cup water
¼ cup fine bread crumbs
½ teaspoon salt
¼ teaspoon pepper

1½ cups boiling water
2 packets brown vegetable bouillon
2 tablespoons lemon juice
⅓ cup brown sugar
¼ cup seedless raisins
6 gingersnaps, crumbled

Combine ground beef, grated onion, and water. Add bread crumbs, salt, and pepper. Form beef mixture into 1-inch balls. Combine boiling water and vegetable bouillon in a Dutch oven. Add lemon juice, brown sugar, raisins, and gingersnaps. Stir around until well blended. Add meat balls and simmer for 1½ hours, stirring occasionally to baste the meatballs with sauce. Makes 6 to 8 servings.

ɔ✧ɔ

Sauerkraut and meatballs? Wait 'til you taste it! A superb combination of sweet and sours to tempt you into eating more than you should.

SAUERKRAUT MEATBALLS

1½ pounds ground beef
1 slice bread
¼ cup water
½ teaspoon salt
¼ teaspoon pepper
¼ teaspoon ginger
2 cups tomato juice
2 8-ounce cans tomato sauce
1 onion, diced
1 one-pound can sauerkraut
½ cup seedless raisins

→ ½ cup brown sugar
6 gingersnaps, crushed

Place chopped meat in a bowl. Soak bread in the water until it can be softened into tiny bits; mix the bread and water through the meat. Add salt, pepper, and ginger; form into 1-inch balls. Pour the tomato juice and tomato sauce into a Dutch oven. Add the onion and sauerkraut; stir all around. Add raisins, brown sugar, and crushed gingersnaps. Add the meatballs; cover and simmer for 1½ hours, stirring occasionally. Serve with cooked rice or noodles. Makes 6 to 8 servings.

꙰

Caraway seeds have an insistant flavor of their own. Try these meatballs for a pleasant departure from your usual fare!

RYE MEATBALLS IN WINE

1 pound ground beef
1 small grated onion
2 tablespoons red wine vinegar
3 slices rye bread
1 cup warm water
1 egg, beaten
1 teaspoon salt
1 teaspoon caraway seeds
¼ teaspoon pepper
½ cup Burgundy wine
½ cup hot water

Combine ground beef with onion and wine vinegar. Soak rye bread in warm water until it is soft and pliable;

shred rye slices and add to meat with water. Add beaten egg, salt, caraway seeds, and pepper. Mix through lightly. Form into 1-inch balls. Combine wine and water together in a deep saucepan. Add meatballs, cover and simmer for 30 minutes. Makes about 2 dozen meatballs, or 4 servings.

)❖)

Spicy meatballs are the star of this spaghetti dish. Nothing fattening about spaghetti either, if you portion-control your intake!

SPAGHETTI WITH MEATBALLS

1 pound ground beef
1 teaspoon salt
⅛ teaspoon pepper
2 tablespoons olive oil
¼ cup chopped onion
1 clove garlic, peeled and minced
2 8-ounce cans tomato sauce
¼ teaspoon Tabasco
1 8-ounce package spaghetti

Sprinkle the beef with salt and pepper; form into small balls. Brown quickly on all sides in oil in skillet. Add onions and garlic when meat is almost brown. Add tomato sauce and Tabasco; cover and simmer 20 to 30 minutes. Cook spaghetti according to directions on package; drain. Turn onto platter and pile meatballs and sauce in center. Makes 4 to 6 servings.

)❖)

Pick peppers of a large and regular formation to make this recipe easy to do. You'll be gratified when you taste the outcome! *11/18/81 Good*

STUFFED GREEN PEPPERS

6 large green peppers
¾ pound ground beef
⅓ cup chopped onion
¼ teaspoon salt
⅛ teaspoon pepper
1 cup cooked rice
2 8-ounce cans tomato sauce with onions

Cut off tops of peppers and remove the membranes and seeds. Wash thoroughly to remove clinging seeds, and then boil in salted water for 2 minutes. Drain. Meanwhile, combine the beef, onion, salt, pepper, and cooked rice. Spoon 2 tablespoons of tomato sauce with onions into this mixture; stuff drained peppers and place them in a small baking pan. Pour remaining tomato sauce over and around the peppers. Bake in a 350°F. oven for 1 hour, basting occasionally with sauce. Makes 6 servings.

))◆))

Does your family turn their noses up when you serve liver the usual way? Try this unique method and watch for their happy response!

LIVER FRICASSEE

1½ pounds calves liver, cut into long strips
1 onion, sliced thin

2 tablespoons corn oil
⅓ cup sherry
1 20-ounce can stewed tomatoes
½ teaspoon sweet basil
½ teaspoon salt
⅛ teaspoon pepper
¼ teaspoon garlic powder
3 cups hot cooked rice

Brown liver stips and onion in oil, using a large skillet. Add wine and simmer for several minutes. Add stewed tomatoes, sweet basil, salt, pepper, and garlic powder; stir. Cover and simmer for 20 minutes, until liver is soft and tender. Remove cover and let sauce thicken. Serve over hot cooked rice. Makes 6 servings.

)◊)

Are you looking for a sure-to-please new party casserole?

The fruity flavored topping on this sliced tongue turns it into an excellent buffet offering.

PICKLED TONGUE WITH APRICOT GLAZE

1 pickled tongue, about 4 pounds
1 one-pound can apricot halves
½ teaspoon cinnamon

In a heavy saucepan, cover tongue with water and cook for 2½ to 3 hours, or until tender. Remove from water and pull off skin; remove any small bones and gristle that may be on the end. Cool. Then slice and place in a flat roasting pan. Put contents of the can of apricots in a blender and chop fine. Add cinnamon. Spread this mixture over the top of the tongue slices and bake at 300°F. for one hour. Makes 6 to 8 servings.

This is the more conventional way to serve sliced tongue. It has a sweet and sour raisin sauce to enhance the pickled meat!

SWEET AND SOUR TONGUE

1 pickled tongue, about 4 pounds
½ cup brown sugar
1 teaspoon mustard
1 tablespoon flour
2 tablespoons wine vinegar
2 tablespoons lemon juice
1 cup water
¼ cup seedless raisins

In a heavy saucepan, cover tongue with water and cook for 2½ to 3 hours, or until tender. Remove from water and pull off skin; remove any small bones and gristle that may be on the end. Cool. Then slice. In a saucepan, mix the brown sugar, mustard, and flour together. Stir in the vinegar, lemon juice, and water. Add the raisins. Simmer over low heat until sauce is thickened and raisins are soft and plump; stir constantly. Spoon hot sauce over tongue slices and serve. Makes 6 to 8 servings.

Veal, being a younger animal product, has less fat and is therefore healthier to eat. Here it is smothered in a pineapple-based barbecue sauce!

VEAL STEAKS WITH BARBECUE SAUCE

6 shoulder veal steaks
½ cup flour
½ teaspoon salt
¼ teaspoon garlic salt
2 tablespoons corn oil
1 8-ounce can tomato sauce
1 8¾-ounce can pineapple tidbits
1 green pepper, cut in chunks
⅓ cup brown sugar
¼ teaspoon ginger

Dredge veal steaks in a mixture of the flour, salt, and garlic salt. Heat corn oil in a skillet; quickly brown the veal steaks on both sides and remove from pan to a flat casserole. Combine tomato sauce, pineapple tidbits (including juice), green pepper (with seeds and membranes removed), brown sugar and ginger in a small saucepan. Simmer this mixture for 5 minutes; then pour over the veal steaks. Bake casserole in a 350°F. oven for 30 minutes, or until veal is tender. Makes 6 servings.

꙲꙳꙲

This is a fatty, bony cut of meat, and needs a stuffing to stretch the number of people you can serve. Some cuts are meatier than others, so try to make a good selection when you make your purchase. You'll get raves over the lemon-rice stuffing!

BREAST OF VEAL WITH LEMON–RICE STUFFING

1 breast of veal, about 4 pounds
2 cups cooked rice

⅓ cup seedless raisins
2 tablespoons minced parsley
1 teaspoon grated lemon rind
½ teaspoon basil
½ teaspoon salt
⅛ teaspoon pepper
½ teaspoon paprika
¼ teaspoon garlic salt

Have butcher slit a pocket into the breast of veal for stuffing. Combine cooked rice, raisins, parsley, lemon rind, basil, salt, and pepper. Stuff into veal pocket. Place breast of veal in a roasting pan; sprinkle exposed surface with paprika and garlic salt. Roast in a 350°F. oven for 2 to 2½ hours, or until browned and tender. Makes 6 servings.

)+>)

If you want to serve this as barbecued ribs, rather than a barbecued roast, cut the roast into 2-rib portions and then proceed with the recipe. Succulent!

BARBECUED BREAST OF VEAL ROAST

1 large breast of veal
½ cup chili sauce
¼ cup water
¼ cup lemon juice
1 small onion, chopped fine
2 teaspoons Worcestershire sauce
1 teaspoon prepared mustard
1 teaspoon brown sugar
¼ teaspoon chili powder

Arrange breast of veal in a flat baking pan. Combine the remaining ingredients in a saucepan and simmer for 5 minutes, stirring occasionally. Then pour this barbecue sauce over the breast of veal and place in a 350°F. oven for about 2½ hours, or until tender. Baste occasionally. Makes 6 servings.

)〉◦〈(

And here's a barbecue sauce with a fruity flavor! Serve it with rice and a wonderful tossed salad.

BREAST OF VEAL WITH FRUITY BARBECUE SAUCE

1 breast of veal, about 4 pounds
1 8-ounce can tomato sauce
½ cup apricot preserves
1 teaspoon soy sauce
1 teaspoon brown sugar
1 teaspoon minced onion
½ teaspoon prepared mustard
½ teaspoon salt
⅛ teaspoon ground ginger

Arrange breast of veal in a flat roasting pan. Combine the remaining ingredients in a small saucepan; simmer for 5 minutes. Pour over breast of veal. Cover pan with foil and bake for 2 hours in a 350°F. oven; then uncover pan and bake for 30 minutes more, or until tender. Makes 4 servings.

)〉◦〈(

No fat to sear the meat first? Not necessary in this Hungarian-inspired paprikash dish! Healthier cooking often tastes better too.

VEAL PAPRIKASH WITH NOODLES

2 pounds cubed lean shoulder of veal
2 tablespoons paprika
3 onions, sliced thin
2 tablespoons minced parsley
1 green pepper, seeded and diced fine
½ teaspoon salt
2 cups beef bouillon
½ cup white wine (optional)
1½ tablespoons cornstarch
8 ounces wide noodles
½ teaspoon caraway seeds

Put veal into a small Dutch oven or casserole that has a tight-fitting cover. Add paprika, and stir through to coat the meat. Add onion slices, parsley, green pepper, and salt. Pour bouillon and wine around the meat. Cover tightly and cook in a 325°F. oven for about 2 hours, or until fork tender. Stir cornstarch with a small amount of water until dissolved; then add some of the hot gravy and return the entire mixture to the cooked meat and gravy. Heat for a few moments on top of the stove, stirring constantly, until the gravy is slightly thickened. Cook noodles as directed on the package; drain and sprinkle with caraway seeds. Serve with the veal and gravy. Makes 6 servings.

sed red inst of green pepper, no doubt not as tasty, iled noodles w mineral salt — didn't use enuf — oo bland.

Trim off excess fat before you broil, and then score diagonally around the edges to prevent chops from curling up. Wait until you taste this snappy sauce!

APRICOT–GLAZED SHOULDER LAMB CHOPS

6 large shoulder lamb chops
½ cup canned apricot nectar
¼ teaspoon ginger

Arrange lamb chops on a broiling rack. Combine apricot nectar with ginger; spoon half of the mixture over the chops. Broil for 4 minutes. Turn chops and spoon remaining mixture over them; broil for 4 minutes longer or until desired doneness is achieved. Makes 6 servings.

❧

A good way to soak meat in a marinade is to place a plastic bag into a small deep bowl, fill it with the sauce and then the meat. Fasten the top of the bag closed and you can change the position of the sauce easily by shifting the bag around every so often.

MARINATED LAMB CHOPS

1 cup tomato puree
2 tablespoons chopped onion
1 tablespoon prepared horseradish
1 tablespoon Worcestershire sauce
¼ cup wine vinegar
½ teaspoon salt
⅛ teaspoon pepper
1½ teaspoons sugar
8 lamb chops

Combine the tomato puree, chopped onion, horseradish, and Worcestershire sauce. Stir in vinegar, salt, pepper, and sugar. Marinate (soak) lamb chops in this mixture for several hours; then remove chops from the marinade and broil 6 to 8 minutes on each side. Baste with remaining marinade if desired. Makes 8 servings.

꠸✢꠸

Another meal-in-a-pot recipe that will bring you compliments! It's the kind of dish you may want to double to provide for seconds.

LAMB RISOTTO

4 large lamb shoulder chops
¼ teaspoon salt
⅛ teaspoon pepper
2 tablespoons corn oil
1 onion, sliced thin
1 green pepper, slivered
1 cup long grain rice
1 tomato, cut into wedges
2 cups bouillon
¾ teaspoon oregano
½ teaspoon salt
¼ teaspoon pepper

Season lamb chops with salt and pepper and broil for 12 to 14 minutes, turning once. Meanwhile, heat oil in pan and add onion and green pepper; cook until tender. Add rice and stir until rice is coated and golden. Then add tomato, bouillon, oregano, salt and pepper; bring to a boil, then cover and simmer for 14 minutes or until rice is tender. Spoon onto platter and top with broiled chops. Makes 4 servings.

꠸✢꠸

Be sure to trim this fatty cut very well, and then let the broiler melt out the rest. All should be lean, crisp, and very brown. Finger-lickin good!

BARBECUED LAMB RIBS

4 pounds lamb ribs, trimmed of excess fat
1 8-ounce can tomato sauce with mushrooms
3 tablespoons soy sauce
2 tablespoons brown sugar
½ teaspoon ground ginger
¼ teaspoon pepper
1 clove garlic, crushed
¼ cup white wine

Place lamb ribs on a broiling pan. Combine tomato sauce, soy sauce, brown sugar, ginger, pepper, garlic, and white wine in a small saucepan; simmer for 4 minutes. Spoon some of the sauce over the ribs. Broil for 5 minutes. Turn and spoon remaining sauce over ribs. Broil until crisp and browned. Makes 4 servings.

⟫✦⟫

Ask for lean meat when you order the cubed lamb, otherwise cook in advance and chill to be able to remove the hardened fat that rises to the top. Simple techniques do insure healthier eating!

LAMB STEW

2 tablespoons olive oil
2 pounds lamb, cut in 1-inch cubes
1 clove garlic, minced

1 medium onion, chopped
1½ teaspoons salt
¼ teaspoon pepper
1 bay leaf
1 whole clove
3 tablespoons chopped parsley
½ teaspoon powdered saffron
½ teaspoon ground ginger
2 large tomatoes, chopped
½ cup water
4 potatoes, peeled and quartered
4 carrots, scraped and cut in chunks
2 sweet green peppers, seeded and cut in chunks

Heat olive oil in a deep heavy saucepan; add lamb cubes and brown on all sides. Add garlic, chopped onion, salt, pepper, bay leaf, clove, parsley, saffron, ginger, and chopped tomatoes. Cook and stir for a few minutes; then add water, potatoes, carrots, and green peppers. Cover and simmer for 1 hour or until lamb and vegetables are tender. Serve on rice or noodles. Makes 8 servings.

꒰꒱

Here's a way of cooking dried white beans right along with the roast, after some preliminary work has been done. The reciprocal flavors achieve a rare good taste!

ROAST SHOULDER OF LAMB WITH BEAN SAUCE

½ pound dried white beans
3 pounds boneless shoulder of lamb, rolled and tied
½ teaspoon salt
¼ teaspoon pepper
¼ teaspoon paprika

1 onion, chopped
1 clove garlic, minced
2 tablespoons chopped parsley
½ teaspoon thyme
½ bay leaf
2 tablespoons olive oil
1 one-pound can tomatoes

Soak the beans overnight, drain and parboil; then simmer until tender. Arrange lamb roast in a flat casserole; sprinkle with salt, pepper, and paprika and place in a 325°F. oven for 2½ hours. Meanwhile, cook onion, garlic, parsley, thyme, and bay leaf in olive oil in a skillet until onion is golden. Then add tomatoes and simmer for 15 minutes. Add cooked beans and simmer for 15 minutes longer. Then remove lamb roast from oven and place this mixture around it in the casserole; return to oven for 15 minutes. Makes 6 to 8 servings.

)♦)

Stuffed peppers can be made with lamb too! This version has a Mid-East flavor and is easy to do.

LAMB STUFFED PEPPERS

5 green peppers
2 cups boiling water
1 pound ground lamb
¾ cup chopped onions
1 clove garlic, minced
1 tablespoon dried mint leaves, crumbled
1½ teaspoons salt
1 cup bouillon
1 cup bread crumbs

½ cup seedless raisins
½ cup chopped nuts
1 tomato, cut into 10 wedges

Cut green peppers in half and remove seeds and stems. Cook in boiling water for 5 minutes, or until tender but still firm. Drain and arrange in a baking pan, hollow side up. Combine lamb, onion, garlic, mint, and salt in a skillet; cook until lamb is brown and onion tender. Drain excess grease. Stir bouillon into lamb mixture. Stir in bread crumbs, raisins, and nuts; mix well. Fill each pepper with this mixture. Press a wedge of tomato into the center of each stuffed pepper. Cover and bake in a 350°F. oven for 45 minutes, then remove cover and bake an additional 15 minutes. Makes 10 servings.

)❖)❋

These broiled lamb balls are made in shish kebab style, with pineapple and green peppers alternating on the skewers. A tangy glaze covers all as it nestles into beds of hot fluffy rice!

GINGER LAMB WITH RICE

1 pound ground lamb
1 egg, beaten
1 teaspoon garlic salt
⅛ teaspoon pepper
½ cup finely crushed gingersnaps
1 8½-ounce can sliced pineapple, quartered
1 large green pepper, cut in 1-inch pieces
½ cup catsup
2 tablespoons brown sugar
1 teaspoon dry mustard

1 tablespoon lemon juice
¼ teaspoon ginger
3 cups hot cooked rice

Combine lamb, egg, garlic salt, pepper, and ginger-snaps. Mix well; form into 1½-inch balls. Alternate meatballs, pineapple, and green pepper on skewers. Brush with glaze made by combining catsup, brown sugar, dry mustard, lemon juice, and ginger together. Broil 7 to 8 minutes on each side, basting occasionally with the remaining glaze mixture. Serve over beds of fluffy rice. Makes 6 servings.

ⅅ✥ⅅ

9. Vegetable Variety

While vegetables need not present any animal or dairy fat problem, often the method of preparation most commonly used is to cream the vegetables before serving them. This is a "no-no" in healthier cookery unless you use methods like those in this chapter. Color, texture, and taste play an important role when selecting vegetables to balance a meal. Here is a stimulating variety from which to choose.

))•))

This method is really teaching you to "blanch" the asparagus before proceeding with the cooking. It assures you of that fresh green color rather than the faded color of overboiling!

BLANCHED ASPARAGUS

1 bunch fresh asparagus
½ teaspoon salt

Boiling water
Iced water
Hollandaise Sauce

Wash and trim asparagus, cutting off tough ends too. Add salt to boiling water and submerge asparagus for 2 minutes; then plunge asparagus into a pan of icy water. This action will keep the asparagus green during further cooking. When ready to serve, again cook asparagus in boiling water for 10 minutes, or until tender. Drain and serve with Hollandaise Sauce, below. Makes 6 servings.

))⬦))

A wire whip, or whisk as it is sometimes called, is a necessity in keeping this sauce smooth during preparation. Serve this elegant sauce over asparagus, broccoli, green beans, or cauliflower, for a supreme finishing touch!

HOLLANDAISE SAUCE

⅓ cup corn oil margarine, softened
2 egg yolks
1 tablespoon lemon juice
1 tablespoon hot water
¼ teaspoon salt

Cream margarine in a double boiler top. With a wire whip gradually beat in egg yolks, then lemon juice, and then water. Place over hot (not boiling) water; cook, beating constantly with whip, until thickened. Stir in salt. Remove from hot water; cover until ready to use. Do not hold more than 1 hour. Whip briskly before serving. Makes about ½ cup.

Note: If sauce becomes too thick or separates, beat in

1 tablespoon hot water, 1 teaspoon at a time, until sauce becomes smooth again.

)•*•)

For those who think that brussels sprouts are a dull vegetable, try this perky way of preparation and change your mind with the first bite. Seasonings and parsley add flavorful touches!

BRUSSELS SPROUTS

1 10-ounce package frozen Brussels sprouts
1 cup water
½ teaspoon salt
→ ½ teaspoon sugar
⅛ teaspoon pepper
1 tablespoon corn oil margarine
1 teaspoon chopped parsley

Cut sprouts in half lengthwise and place in a saucepan with the water, salt, sugar, and pepper. Cook for 5 minutes, or until sprouts are tender but not mushy. Drain. Add margarine and parsley, toss lightly and serve. Makes 4 servings.

)•*•)

While one vegetable is often good, two together are often better. Try this carrot-mushroom duo with tarragon flavor!

FRESH CARROTS AND MUSHROOMS TARRAGON

8 to 10 medium carrots (1 pound)
1 cup water

1 teaspoon dried leaf tarragon
½ teaspoon salt
2 tablespoons corn oil margarine
¼ pound fresh mushrooms, sliced

Pare carrots and cut into ¼-inch crosswise slices. Place in medium saucepan; add water, tarragon and salt. Cover and cook over medium heat 20 to 30 minutes, until tender. While carrots are cooking, heat margarine in a small skillet; add mushrooms and cook until tender. If there is much water left in the pan with the carrots, drain the carrots. Add mushrooms to carrots and mix lightly. Make 4 to 6 servings.

))•>))

Carrots are known to brighten up your cheeks and improve your eyesight. Here's a way to wake up your taste buds too!

ORANGE GLAZED CARROT STICKS

8 to 10 medium carrots (1 pound)
2 tablespoons corn oil margarine
¼ cup chopped onion
⅓ cup packed light brown sugar
½ cup orange juice
½ teaspoon salt

Pare carrots and cut into sticks by cutting in half lengthwise, then into lengthwise quarters and eighths. In a large skillet, cook the carrots, covered, in a small amount of water until tender. Remove carrots from skillet. Heat margarine in same skillet; add onion and cook until tender. Stir in brown sugar and orange juice; simmer 5 minutes.

Add cooked carrots, sprinkle with salt, and spoon sauce over carrots until glazed and heated. Makes 4 to 6 servings.

)❖)

You'll find extra flavor in this recipe when you add a bouillon cube to the cooking water. A simple vegetable made extra-tasty!

TENDER CARROTS

1 bunch slender carrots, scraped and sliced thin
½ cup water
1 bouillon cube
¼ teaspoon salt
¼ teaspoon sugar

Place sliced carrots into a heavy saucepan. Add water, bouillon cube, salt and sugar. Cook for 15 minutes, or until tender. Drain and serve.

)❖)

If you have time, start from scratch with a bunch of carrots as you are directed to do in the preceding recipe for Tender Carrots. Then proceed to make this quicker version below!

PECAN GLAZED CARROTS

2 one-pound cans sliced carrots
2 tablespoons corn oil margarine
½ cup carrot liquid
¾ cup light brown sugar

Dash salt
½ cup coarsely chopped pecans

Heat canned carrots in own liquid, reserving ½ cup liquid for the sauce. In a saucepan, combine margarine, carrot liquid, brown sugar, and salt. Bring to a boil; simmer for 2 minutes. Add pecans. Pour over drained carrots and stir gently. Serves 6 to 8.

)⊱)

Float a slice of rye bread in the pot to cut down on cooking aroma. An old wives' trick that really works!

SWEET 'N SOUR CABBAGE

1 medium head cabbage
¼ cup corn oil margarine
→ ¼ cup light corn syrup
⅓ cup vinegar
Dash pepper
Dash paprika
1 teaspoon caraway seeds

Shred cabbage and cook in water until tender but still crisp; drain. Melt margarine in a small saucepan. Stir in light corn syrup, vinegar, pepper and paprika. Bring to a boil. Add caraway seeds. Pour hot sauce over drained cabbage; toss. Serve at once. Makes 6 to 8 servings.

)⊱)

This red cabbage is a natural to serve with Sauerbraten or any other pot roast. Apples give it a tart flavor, and sweets and sours do the rest!

RED CABBAGE

1 medium-sized red cabbage, shredded
4 apples, pared and sliced
⅓ cup brown sugar
2 tablespoons red wine vinegar
½ cup water
1 teaspoon salt
½ teaspoon basil

Place cabbage and apples in a heavy saucepan with a tight-fitting lid. Add brown sugar, vinegar, and water. Add salt and basil; stir. Cover tightly and simmer for about 2 hours, adding more water if needed. Makes 6 to 8 servings.

)◆)

If you're looking for a way to serve celery as a captivating vegetable, here's the recipe that does it! The crunch the celery loses in the cooking is replaced by slivers of almonds.

CELERY AMANDINE

1 medium bunch celery, cut in 1-inch pieces
½ teaspoon salt
½ teaspoon sugar
1 sprig fresh parsley
2 cups chicken soup
1 tablespoon corn oil margarine
1 tablespoon slivered almonds

Place celery in a saucepan. Add salt, sugar, and fresh parsley. Add chicken soup; cover and cook for about 15 minutes, or until celery is tender and chicken soup has almost evaporated. Add margarine and almonds to hot celery. Serve at once. Makes 6 servings.

)❖)❮

If you wish, just trim the ends of the green beans and leave them whole. Either way, you'll relish their flavor!

GREEN BEANS AND TOMATOES

1 pound fresh green beans, trimmed and sliced
2 tomatoes, cut in wedges
1 small onion, diced
½ teaspoon salt
½ teaspoon sugar
⅛ teaspoon pepper
1 bay leaf
1 cup water

Place green beans in a heavy saucepan. Add remaining ingredients and cook until beans are tender, about 15 minutes. Drain and serve. Makes 6 servings.

)❖)❮

Serve pickled green beans instead of a salad. Great bait for a fish dinner!

PICKLED GREEN BEANS

1 pound whole green beans
2 whole pimientos (canned)
1 sliced onion
¼ cup olive oil
2 tablespoons wine vinegar

→ 1 teaspoon sugar
½ teaspoon salt
⅛ teaspoon pepper

Cut ends from green beans and wash thoroughly. Place in a saucepan with just enough boiling water to cover. Cook for about 20 minutes, or until tender. Drain. Chop pimientos and add to beans. Add separated onion rings. Stir together oil, vinegar, sugar, salt, and pepper; pour over green beans and toss until all are well coated. Chill and serve. Makes 6 servings.

)⟩❖⟨(

These are named for the famous orange-growing state. Adding molasses along with undiluted frozen orange concentrate gives a unique flavor. A sensational kick to plain old baked beans!

FLORIDA BAKED BEANS

1 one-pound can baked beans
2 tablespoons frozen orange juice concentrate, thawed
1 tablespoon molasses

Combine baked beans, orange juice concentrate and molasses. Heat in a saucepan on top of range or turn into a casserole and heat in a 375°F. oven for 30 minutes. Makes 3 to 4 servings.

)⟩❖⟨(

If you decide to start with fresh broccoli, take the time to scrape the stems with a food peeler. Then cut in quarters lengthwise. It will be tender with less cooking time, and tastier too!

BROCCOLI WITH LEMON SAUCE

2 10-ounce packages frozen broccoli
2 tablespoons corn oil margarine
2 tablespoons lemon juice
½ teaspoon salt

Cook frozen broccoli according to package directions, then drain. Melt margarine in a saucepan. Remove from heat and stir in lemon juice and salt. Pour over the cooked broccoli and serve. Makes 6 servings.

〉〉✧〉〉

These are often called Harvard beets, but they couldn't taste any smarter no matter what you name them. It's the sweet and sour balance that gladdens your palate!

SWEET 'N' SOUR BEETS

1 one-pound can sliced beets
1 tablespoon cornstarch
1 tablespoon corn oil margarine
1 tablespoon vinegar
1 teaspoon sugar

Drain beet juice into a saucepan. Stir in cornstarch until completely smooth. Stir in margarine, vinegar, and sugar; cook and stir constantly until margarine melts and mixture thickens. Add beets and heat through. Serve at once. Makes 4 servings.

〉〉✧〉〉

What a little sprig of fresh dill can do! Try one with these lima beans to stimulate appreciation.

DILLED LIMA BEANS

1 10-ounce package frozen lima beans
½ teaspoon salt
→ ½ teaspoon sugar
Dash pepper
1 sprig fresh dill

Place frozen lima beans in a saucepan. Add salt, sugar, pepper, and fresh dill. Add 1 cup boiling water. Heat until water reboils; then simmer for 15 minutes, or until beans are tender. Drain and serve. Makes 4 servings.

)⬧)

Eggplant has a nondescript personality when left on its own, but here it is smothered with tomatoes and seasonings that turn it into a delicious offering. Great with veal!

EGGPLANT AND TOMATOES

1 eggplant, weighing about 1 pound
1 one-pound can stewed tomatoes
½ teaspoon salt
→ 1 teaspoon sugar
½ teaspoon celery seed

Peel and dice eggplant. Empty stewed tomatoes into a large skillet. Add diced eggplant, salt, sugar, and celery seed. Stir. Cover and simmer for 15 minutes, or until eggplant is tender. Makes 6 servings.

)⬧)

The only way to eat freshly picked peas is raw from the

pod! But if they've been picked more than five minutes before, try this recipe for sweet peas rosemary.

SWEET PEAS ROSEMARY

2 pounds peas, shelled
2 cups boiling water
½ teaspoon salt
1 teaspoon sugar
¼ teaspoon rosemary

Place shelled peas in a saucepan; cover with boiling water. Add salt, sugar, and rosemary. Bring to a boil, then lower heat and simmer for 15 to 20 minutes, or just until peas are tender. Makes 4 servings.

)❀)

Here's a healthier way to make a white sauce. Vegetable margarine and skim milk get the saturated fat out and the rest of the recipe gets the taste back in!

CREAMED SPINACH

2 10-ounce packages frozen chopped spinach
1 small onion, diced fine
½ teaspoon salt
¼ teaspoon nutmeg
1 tablespoon corn oil margarine
1 tablespoon flour
1 cup skim milk

Place spinach, onion, salt, and nutmeg in a saucepan. Cover the bottom of the saucepan with ½ inch of water. Cook for 10 minutes, or until spinach is soft; then drain well. Melt margarine in a small saucepan; stir in flour, and then gradually stir in milk. Cook and stir until mixture bubbles and thickens. Fold this sauce through the spinach. Makes 6 to 8 servings.

꒐꒐

Don't overlook frozen orange juice concentrate as a powerful flavoring agent. Here it makes a sauce triumph!

SPINACH WITH ORANGE SAUCE

1 10-ounce package frozen chopped spinach
2 tablespoons frozen orange juice concentrate, thawed
2 tablespoons corn oil margarine

Cook spinach as directed on the package. Drain. Combine orange juice concentrate and corn oil margarine in a small saucepan; heat until margarine melts and mixture is warm. Pour over cooked spinach and serve. Makes 3 to 4 servings.

꒐꒐

It takes just a little know-how to bake a great tomato dish. Do add the bit of basil, it has just the oomph needed!

BAKED TOMATOES

6 medium-sized tomatoes
¼ teaspoon salt
⅛ teaspoon pepper
⅛ teaspoon basil
2 tablespoons chopped onion

Wash tomatoes and cut off a thin slice at the top (stem end). Place tomatoes in a small casserole, season with salt, pepper, and basil. Top with chopped onion. Add enough water to cover the bottom of the casserole. Bake in a 375°F. oven for about 15 minutes, or until tomatoes are soft but still firm. Makes 6 servings.

)❉)

Zucchini made this way has a captivating flavor. Serve it with a bland dish to give zest to your meal!

STEWED ZUCCHINI

2 large zucchini squash, sliced ½ inch thick
1 onion, sliced thin
1 one-pound can tomatoes, including juice
½ teaspoon thyme
½ teaspoon garlic powder
½ teaspoon salt
¼ teaspoon pepper

Place zucchini and onion slices in a heavy saucepan. Add tomatoes. Season with thyme, garlic powder, salt and pepper. Cover and simmer for 15 minutes, or until zucchini is tender. Makes 4 to 6 servings.

)❉)

Acorn squash has a similar flavor to sweet potato. Made this way it becomes a major part of your meal!

BAKED ACORN SQUASH

3 acorn squash
2 cups applesauce

½ cup brown sugar
⅓ cup seedless raisins
⅓ cup broken walnuts

Scrub squash; cut in half lengthwise and remove the seeds and stringy portions. Combine applesauce, sugar, raisins, and nuts; spoon this mixture into cavities in squash halves. Place squash in a baking dish and add enough water to cover the bottom of the dish. Cover (with foil if necessary) and bake in a 400°F. oven for 1 hour or until squash is fork tender. Remove cover and bake for 20 minutes more. Makes 6 servings.

))•))

Fresh mushrooms ooze their subtle flavor into the surrounding vegetables and rice. Here's a vegetable mold worthy of a party table!

RICE AND MUSHROOM MOLD

2 tablespoons corn oil
½ pound fresh mushrooms, sliced
1 onion, diced
1 green pepper, diced
1 one-pound can tomatoes
½ cup water
1 cup uncooked rice
2 tablespoons chopped parsley
1 teaspoon salt

Heat corn oil in a large deep skillet. Sauté mushrooms, onion, and green pepper until limp. Add tomatoes and water, stir, and bring to a boil. Add rice, parsley, and salt. Turn heat low, cover and cook for 30 minutes, or until rice is tender. Pack into a lightly greased 1-quart ring mold and turn out onto a platter. Makes 6 servings.

)✦)

For delicious rice, bake it in broth! The simple way to do it is described below.

BAKED RICE

1 cup uncooked rice
2 cups boiling chicken broth (fat free)
½ teaspoon salt
2 tablespoons minced fresh parsley

Combine rice, broth, salt, and parsley, in a greased casserole. Stir. Cover with foil or a tight fitting lid and place in a 375°F. oven. Bake for 30 minutes. Makes 6 servings.

)✦)

Everyone will make a fuss over this vegetable-fruit concoction. It's a version of tsimmes that will tickle your tonsils!

TSIMMES

4 white potatoes, peeled and quartered
2 sweet potatoes, peeled and quartered
4 carrots, scraped and sliced
1 one-pound jar applesauce with apricots
1 tablespoon brown sugar

Cover white potatoes, sweet potatoes, and carrots with water; bring to a boil and then simmer until vegetables are tender. Drain. Combine vegetables and applesauce with apricots; sprinkle brown sugar over top. Bake in a 350°F. oven for 20 minutes. Makes 6 servings.

)‣)

Peanut oil is a flavorful unsaturated fat product and a perfect selection for making potato pancakes. Fry it, you'll like it!

POTATO PANCAKES

4 large peeled potatoes
1 small onion
1 egg, beaten
2 tablespoons matzo meal
½ teaspoon salt
½ cup peanut oil

Grate potatoes and onion into a deep bowl. Stir in egg and matzo meal. Add salt. Heat oil in a large skillet. Drop batter by large spoonfuls into the hot oil. Fry on one side and then turn. Serve with applesauce or Prune-Apple Pancake Sauce on page 184. Makes 6 servings.

)‣)

Somehow Friday night dinner and potato kugel seem to go together. But with this new way, there are no after effects from saturated chicken fat! Still tastes very good, and so much healthier for you and yours.

POTATO KUGEL

6 large potatoes
1 small onion, grated

3 eggs
¼ teaspoon salt
⅛ teaspoon pepper
2 tablespoons flour
¼ cup softened margarine

Grate potatoes and onion and drain well. Beat in eggs, salt, and pepper. Add flour. Add softened margarine and mix well. Pour into a greased 1-quart casserole and bake in a 350°F. oven for 35 minutes, or until top is lightly browned. Makes 6 to 8 servings.

)❖)

Use canned sweet potatoes, packed in water, if you need a faster start with these orange mashed sweet potatoes. Be sure to heat them before mashing so the margarine will melt!

ORANGE MASHED SWEET POTATOES

4 sweet potatoes, cooked and peeled
3 tablespoons corn oil margarine
2 tablespoons orange juice
⅛ teaspoon salt
⅛ teaspoon nutmeg

Mash hot sweet potatoes. Add margarine, orange juice, salt and nutmeg. Beat until fluffy. Serve immediately. Makes 4 servings.

)❖)

10. Crispy Salads

)✥

Whether your salad is suspended in gelatin or smothered in dressing, every recipe in this chapter has been planned to offer the healthier way to make it. Many are complete meals in one. Others are intended as a side dish to a main course. You'll find combinations of vegetables, fruits, and nuts that will excite your cooking imagination, while showing you how to eliminate saturated fats.

)✥)

You'll find bulgur cracked wheat in your health food store. The rest of the ingredients are available in supermarkets and all combine into a mighty filling health salad. Do the dressing in an electric blender, if you prefer!

CRACKED WHEAT HEALTH SALAD

6/80 - To improve taste added tomatoes, green pepper, Accent

1 cup bulgur cracked wheat
2 cups water
½ teaspoon salt

See p 95 - Jewish Low-Cholesterol Cookbook.

2 tablespoons dried mint leaves, crushed
1 cup thinly sliced scraped carrots
1 15½-ounce can garbanzo beans, drained
1 tablespoon chopped pimiento
2 green onions, chopped
¼ cup parsley, finely chopped
1 cup shredded iceberg lettuce
¼ cup olive oil
Juice of 1 lemon
¼ teaspoon salt

Cook bulgur wheat in saucepan with salted water as directed on the package. Pour cooked bulgur into mixing bowl. Mix in mint, carrots, garbanzo beans, pimiento, parsley, onions, and shredded lettuce. Pour oil and lemon juice over all. Sprinkle with salt and toss. Serve with Avocado Yoghurt Dressing below. Makes 6 to 8 servings.

Avocado Yoghurt Dressing:
1 cup plain yoghurt
2 tablespoons mashed ripe avocado
Dash of Tabasco sauce
⅛ teaspoon garlic salt

Combine yoghurt and mashed avocado; add Tabasco sauce and garlic salt. Serve as a dressing for Health Salad above.

)❖)

Do make this salad in advance so it can be marinated for several days before using. Keep in a tightly covered jar and refrigerate until ready to eat.

PICKLED VEGETABLE SALAD

1 small head cabbage, sliced thin
4 carrots, scraped and sliced thin
2 cucumbers, peeled and sliced thin
1 Bermuda onion, sliced thin
1 green pepper, seeded and diced
½ cup salad oil
½ cup vinegar
¼ cup sugar
½ teaspoon salt
½ teaspoon celery seed

Combine the vegetables together in a deep bowl. Then stir the oil, vinegar, sugar, salt, and celery seed together and pour over the vegetables. Toss and turn until well coated with the liquid. Cover tightly and store in the refrigerator for 2 or 3 days before using. Makes 8 servings.

꘡❖꘡

Use regular white onion if you wish, but the red onion is sweeter and more colorful. Run the tines of a fork down the sides of the peeled cucumbers for a slightly ruffled-looking edge when sliced!

PICKLED CUCUMBER SALAD

2 cucumbers, peeled and thinly sliced
1 small red onion, thinly sliced
¼ cup red wine vinegar
1 tablespoon olive oil
½ tablespoon salt

¼ teaspoon pepper
1 teaspoon sugar

Place sliced cucumbers and onion in a small deep bowl. Combine vinegar, oil, salt, pepper, and sugar; pour over cucumbers and let marinate for several hours before serving. Makes 6 servings.

)❖)

This Russian dressing cuts down on mayonnaise but not on taste! Use a wire whisk to blend well.

HEARTS OF LETTUCE WITH RUSSIAN DRESSING

1 large head iceberg lettuce
¼ cup mayonnaise
¼ cup plain yoghurt
2 tablespoons chili sauce

Cut head of lettuce into 6 or 8 wedges. Combine mayonnaise, yoghurt, and chili sauce; blend well. Pour about a tablespoon of sauce over each wedge of lettuce. Makes 6 to 8 servings.

)❖)

The mushrooms should be super-fresh and super-white to be sliced raw in a salad. This combination is irresistible!

MUSHROOM SALAD

½ head romaine lettuce
½ head iceberg lettuce
¼ pound fresh mushrooms, sliced thin
¼ cup olive oil

1 tablespoon wine vinegar
¼ teaspoon dry mustard

Tear romaine and iceberg lettuce into a salad bowl. Add sliced mushrooms. Combine olive oil, vinegar, and dry mustard; shake well to emulsify; pour over the salad. Toss and serve. Makes 6 to 8 servings.

)+>)

Use fresh dill for the flavorful dressing, if you can find it. Slice the tomatoes extra-thick and pour the dressing on just before serving!

TOMATO ONION SALAD

3 large beefsteak tomatoes
1 large green pepper
1 Bermuda onion
1 teaspoon dillweed, minced
¼ cup olive oil
1 tablespoon wine vinegar

Slice tomatoes, green pepper, and onion into rings; arrange attractively on a platter. Combine dillweed, oil, and vinegar; shake vigorously just before pouring on salad. Makes 6 to 8 servings.

)+>)

It's a colorful combination of textures and tastes! If you prefer an oilier dressing, add a little more olive oil to the artichoke jar. Freeze-dried chives should be a welcome addition to your seasoning shelf, if the fresh variety are hard to find.

ARTICHOKE SALAD

1 head iceberg lettuce, shredded
½ small head red cabbage, shredded
1 6-ounce jar pickled artichoke hearts
¼ cup red wine vinegar
1 tablespoon chopped chives

Combine shredded lettuce and red cabbage. Drain oil from artichoke hearts and shake well with wine vinegar. Pour over lettuce. Top with artichoke hearts and chopped chives. Toss lightly and serve. Makes 8 servings.

)⋗)

Up to now, you've probably been using dairy sour cream for this type of salad. Make a healthier switch to yoghurt, and eliminate the saturated fat altogether!

VEGETABLE SALAD WITH
YOGHURT–CHIVE DRESSING

1 large cucumber, peeled and diced
4 radishes, sliced
1 green pepper, seeded and diced
2 stalks celery, sliced
1 large tomato, cut up
2 cups cottage cheese
1 cup plain yoghurt
2 tablespoons chopped chives

Combine the diced and sliced vegetables into a bowl. Add cottage cheese and stir lightly until cheese and vegetables are mixed through. Stir yoghurt and chives together

and use as dressing for the vegetable-cheese mixture.
Makes 4 servings.

）❖）

Be sure that the raw spinach are crisp young tender
leaves. The old wilted ones must be cooked before serving
for best results. Do trim the raw spinach well, discarding
heavy veins and discolorations!

FRESH SPINACH SALAD

4 cups chopped raw spinach
½ teaspoon seasoned salt
1½ teaspoons wine vinegar
½ teaspoon Tabasco sauce
¾ cup finely chopped celery
¼ cup finely chopped green pepper
2 tablespoons finely chopped onion
2 hard-cooked eggs, chopped
½ cup diced American cheese
¼ cup mayonnaise
¼ cup yoghurt
2 teaspoons horseradish
Lettuce cups

Sprinkle spinach with seasoned salt. Mix vinegar and
Tabasco sauce; toss with spinach. Mix in celery, green
pepper, onion, most of the chopped egg (reserving some
for garnish), and cheese. Stir together the mayonnaise,
yoghurt, and horseradish; toss with spinach mixture. Serve
in lettuce cups, garnished with chopped egg. Makes 8
servings.

）❖）

This is a delicious salad for a luncheon platter, and colorful too. They'll eat it with gusto!

CHOPPED BEET SALAD   7/7/80

2 tablespoons mayonnaise
2 tablespoons yoghurt
2 teaspoons vinegar
1 teaspoon sugar
Dash salt
1 one-pound can beets, drained and chopped
2 hard-cooked eggs, chopped
2 tablespoons finely chopped onion

Stir together the mayonnaise and yoghurt; add vinegar, sugar, and salt. Toss with chopped beets, eggs and onion. Chill. Makes 6 servings.

)⬦)

Here's a natural and sweet fluffy dressing to serve with a Waldorf salad. Try it this healthier way!

YOGHURT WALDORF SALAD

2 apples
½ cup raisins
½ cup broken walnuts
½ cup plain yoghurt
1 tablespoon honey
Lettuce cups

Core apples and cut into bite-sized chunks. Add raisins and walnuts. Beat yoghurt and honey together. Spoon fruit and nut mixture onto lettuce cups. Top with yoghurt-honey dressing. Makes 4 to 6 servings.

)**❖**))

For a lighter dressing, substitute prepared salad dressing for the mayonnaise. Combine it with yoghurt to cut down on fat intake. You'll enjoy the difference!

COLE SLAW

4 cups finely shredded cabbage
¼ cup thinly sliced green pepper
2 tablespoons thinly sliced pimiento
2 scallions, thinly sliced
½ teaspoon salt
¼ cup mayonnaise
¼ cup yoghurt
½ teaspoon sugar

Combine cabbage, green pepper, pimiento, and scallions. Sprinkle with salt. Combine mayonnaise, yoghurt, and sugar; toss through the cabbage mixture. Chill. Makes 6 to 8 servings.

)**❖**))

Celery seed and mustard seed are available in dried forms at your grocer's counter. They give this potato salad a triumphant flavor!

POTATO SALAD

1 tablespoon celery seed
1½ teaspoons mustard seed

3 tablespoons vinegar
½ cup finely chopped green onion
1 tablespoon sugar
1 teaspoon salt
5 cups diced cooked potatoes
2 hard cooked-eggs, chopped
½ cup mayonnaise
½ cup yoghurt

Soak celery seed and mustard seed in vinegar for several hours. Add green onion, sugar, and salt to seed mixture. Add potatoes and eggs and mix lightly. Stir mayonnaise and yoghurt together and toss lightly through potato mixture. Chill thoroughly. Makes 8 to 10 servings.

)▶❖)❖)

This is a lovely vegetable-rice ring to serve hot or cold. It has a piquant flavor and would be a fine addition to a buffet table!

RICE SALAD MOLD

2 cups chicken broth
2 tablespoons tarragon vinegar
½ teaspoon salt
1 cup uncooked rice
½ cup diced cucumber, peeled and seeded
¼ cup finely chopped green pepper
2 tablespoons thinly sliced scallions
2 diced pimientos
¼ teaspoon pepper

Combine broth, vinegar, and salt in a saucepan and bring to a boil; add rice and stir well. Cover, lower heat and simmer about 15 minutes, or until rice is tender. While hot, add cucumber, green pepper, scallions, pimientos, and pepper. Toss lightly until all is mixed well. Spoon into a 1-quart oiled ring mold. Chill several hours to serve cold. To serve hot, simply unmold at once and serve. Makes 6 servings.

)◆)

For a fancier version of tomato surprise, try this tuna-rice salad in tomato wedge cups. Yoghurt and anchovies make a dressing treat!

TUNA–RICE SALAD

4 small tomatoes
1 6½-ounce can tuna, drained
1 cup cold cooked rice
2 tablespoons scallions, finely chopped
2 tablespoons fresh parsley, finely chopped
6 pitted black olives, finely chopped
½ cup yoghurt
2 anchovy fillets, finely chopped (optional)
Lettuce leaves

Cut tomatoes in wedges, being careful not to let the knife cut all the way through. Combine tuna, rice, scallions, parsley, and olives. Stir yoghurt and chopped anchovies together; mix through tuna mixture. Pile into centers of tomatoes. Place each on a lettuce leaf and serve. Makes 4 servings.

)◆)

Macaroni amplifies this garden salad into an important part of the meal. If you prefer a creamier dressing, substitute equal parts of mayonnaise and yoghurt for the olive oil.

MACARONI GARDEN SALAD

8 ounces elbow macaroni
1 green pepper, cut in slivers
2 tomatoes, cut in wedges
3 scallions, sliced thin
1 cucumber, sliced thin
Romain lettuce leaves
¼ cup olive oil
1½ tablespoons wine vinegar
¾ teaspoon salt
⅛ teaspoon pepper
¼ teaspoon dry mustard

Cook macaroni as directed on the package; drain and rinse. Combine with green pepper, tomatoes, scallions, and cucumber. Line a salad bowl with crisp romaine leaves and fill the center with the macaroni mixture. Combine olive oil, vinegar, salt, pepper, and mustard; stir briskly and pour over macaroni salad. Toss and serve. Makes 6 to 8 servings.

)♦)

This is a must for every Passover table, but is a tasty combination to serve on other occasions too. Add honey and wine to the apples as soon as they are chopped, to keep them from turning brown!

CHAROSETH

2 apples
½ cup shelled walnuts
1 tablespoon honey
4 tablespoons Passover sweet red wine
Dash of cinnamon

Leave peel on apples, but remove core and seeds. Chop fine with walnuts. Add honey, wine, and cinnamon and mix well. Serve in a bowl to be passed around the table at the Passover meal. Makes 6 to 8 servings.

)▶◀)

You make this gelatin mold right in the can of pineapple! Pretty enough to eat.

PINEAPPLE–CABBAGE GEL

1 20-ounce can sliced pineapple ←
1 3-ounce package lime gelatin ←
1 cup boiling water
1 cup shredded cabbage

Remove top from can of pineapple and, leaving slices in the can, drain off the juice for use later. Dissolve lime gelatin in a bowl with boiling water; add enough cold water to the pineapple juice to make ¾ cup and add that to the gelatin mixture too. Mix thoroughly. Place shredded cabbage in the center hole of the pineapple in the can. Pour in just enough gelatin mixture to reach the top; pour remaining gelatin into sherbet glasses for another time. Chill. When ready to serve, puncture bottom of can and slide out jelled pineapple. Slice between the pineapple slices, and place each slice on a bed of lettuce. Makes 6 to 8 servings.

)⋅⧫⋅)

This is a wonderful side dish for fish because it adds color and tangy taste to an otherwise bland offering. Cut down on the horseradish if you're not used to its flavor!

BEET AND HORSERADISH MOLD

1 3-ounce package lemon gelatin
1 cup boiling water
1 cup red beet juice, drained from canned beets
1 one-pound can sliced julienne beets, drained
4 tablespoons red horseradish
2 tablespoons lemon juice

Dissolve gelatin in boiling water. Add beet juice. Chill until partially jelled; then stir beets, horseradish, and lemon juice together, and stir into gelatin. Pour entire contents into a ring mold and chill for several hours until firm. Serve with fish or meat dishes. Makes 8 to 10 servings.

)⋅⧫⋅)

Do make this in a glass pie plate if you can so everyone can see the colors as you cut to serve it. It's a most unusual way to make a gelatin mold!

JELLIED PEAR SALAD PIE

1 one-pound can sliced pears
1 3-ounce package lime gelatin

1 cup boiling water
8 large green olives, stuffed with pimento ←

Drain and reserve syrup from pears. Arrange pears attractively in a 9-inch pie pan. Combine gelatin and boiling water, stirring until completely dissolved. Add enough water to pear juice to measure 1 cup; stir into gelatin. Pour gelatin over pears. Slice green olives and place among the pear slices. Chill until firm for several hours. Cut and serve as salad pie-shaped wedges. Makes 6 to 8 servings.

꠫꠶꠫

For a gelatin mold with a creamy appearance, try this Mandarin mint salad mold. The many flavors combine to make a refreshing taste!

MANDARIN MINT SALAD MOLD

1 3-ounce package lime gelatin
1½ cups boiling water
¼ cup mint flavored jelly
¼ cup mayonnaise
¼ cup yoghurt
1 13¼-ounce can crushed pineapple, drained ←
1 11-ounce can Mandarin orange sections, drained and
   cut up
⅓ cup chopped pecans

Dissolve gelatin in 1 cup of boiling water. Dissolve mint flavored jelly in remaining ½ cup boiling water. Combine the two mixtures. Stir in mayonnaise and yoghurt. Chill until slightly thickened. Then stir in crushed pineapple, oranges, and nuts. Pour into a 1-quart mold. Chill for several hours until firm. Makes 8 servings.

)⟡)⟡

Definitely party fare, this mold will be a conversation piece on a buffet table. Just enough sherry to kick things off to a good start!

CHERRY SHERRY MOLD

2 3-ounce packages black cherry gelatin
1 cup boiling water
2 one-pound cans bing cherries, pitted and drained
1 one-pound can crushed pineapple, drained
½ cup sherry wine
½ cup chopped walnuts or pecans

Empty contents of the gelatin packages into a large bowl; stir in boiling water until gelatin is completely dissolved. Pour drained juices from cherries and pineapple into a measuring container; add sherry wine and enough water to make 2½ cups of liquid in all. Stir into gelatin mixture. Add pineapple, cherries, and nuts; pour all into a 2-quart ring mold. Chill for several hours until firm. Makes 10 to 14 servings.

)⟡)⟡

Use this for your next Thanksgiving Day dinner and wait for a shower of compliments. Just a little different way to serve the traditional cranberry sauce!

CRANBERRY NUT MOLD

1 one-pound can whole cranberry sauce
2 cups water

2 3-ounce packages lemon gelatin
1 cup diced celery
1 cup chopped walnuts

Empty cranberry sauce into a saucepan and add water; heat and stir until cranberry sauce is melted and mixture is boiling. Stir in lemon gelatin until gelatin is completely dissolved. Remove from heat and add 1 cup of cold water. Add celery and walnuts. Pour all into a 2-quart ring mold. Chill for several hours until firm. Serve with meat, chicken, or turkey. Makes 10 to 14 servings.

)❖)

11. Breads and Muffins

)▶•

Nothing says "I love you" better than homemade bread! Here is a chapter of lovable loaves and muffins that run the cooking gamut from easy-to-prepare to hard-but-gratifying. They all freeze well, so don't hesitate to double a recipe and store your extra effort in your home freezer for another lazier day. The oohs and ahhs at serving time will be your just reward!

)▶•)

If you have never tried to make challah before, try it just once in your lifetime. For the gladness that fills your heart as you serve this traditional loaf will make the effort very worthwhile!

CHALLAH LOAVES

6 cups unsifted, unbleached flour
1 ounce fresh yeast
1⅓ cups warm water

1 tablespoon sugar
¾ tablespoon kosher salt
Pinch of saffron
3 tablespoons corn oil
3 eggs
Additional corn oil
Poppy seeds

Sift the flour into a large bowl. Crumble the yeast into a small bowl; add warm water and sugar. When it bubbles after a few moments, add salt and saffron. Beat eggs and spoon off 1 tablespoon to use as a glaze for the loaves; add corn oil to the remaining beaten eggs and stir well. Then stir egg mixture into the yeast mixture and quickly stir the combined mixture into the flour until you have a soft ball. Knead this well. Then paint the top of the dough with additional corn oil and cover with a clean cloth. Place in a warm area for 1 hour or until it doubles in bulk. Then punch the dough down and knead again. Divide the dough into 6 parts; form long fat ropes. Pinch one end of three ropes together and braid loosely. Repeat with the second three ropes. Oil two 9 x 5 x 3 inch loaf pans and place one braid of dough in each. Brush with reserved beaten egg and sprinkle with poppy seeds. Bake in a pre-heated 400°F. oven for 45 minutes. Makes 2 loaves.

)‣)

No artificial additives needed to protect this hearty loaf. Once it's on the table there won't be a crumb left!

APPLE–MOLASSES BREAD

½ cup corn oil margarine
1 cup sugar

3 eggs
2 cups sifted flour
1 teaspoon baking powder
½ teaspoon salt
½ teaspoon cinnamon
½ teaspoon nutmeg
1 cup applesauce
¼ cup molasses
1 cup seedless raisins
½ cup chopped pecans

Cream margarine and sugar together. Add eggs, one at a time, beating well after each addition. Sift together flour, baking powder, salt, cinnamon and nutmeg. Combine applesauce and molasses. Add flour mixture, alternating with applesauce mixture, to the egg mixture. Beat well after each addition. Fold in raisins and nuts. Pour into a greased and floured 9 x 5 x 3 inch loaf pan. Bake in a 350°F. oven for 1 hour. Makes 8 slices.

))❖))

You'll love the cheese flavor and the ease of this cornbread. If you want a spread, make sure it's corn oil margarine!

PARMESAN CORNBREAD

3 cups packaged biscuit mix
¾ cup yellow cornmeal
¼ cup sugar
¾ cup grated Parmesan cheese
1½ cups buttermilk
2 eggs, beaten

In a large bowl combine biscuit mix, cornmeal, sugar, and cheese. Combine buttermilk and eggs; add to dry ingredients. Stir just until blended; turn into a greased 9 x 5 x 3 inch loaf pan. Bake in 350°F. oven for 45 to 55 minutes, or until lightly browned. Turn out of pan onto a wire rack to cool. Makes 8 servings.

))•))

A good old breakfast hot cereal comes to the fore in this version of spoon bread. Nutritious and delicious!

FARINA SPOON BREAD

2 cups water
1 teaspoon salt
¾ cup enriched cream of farina
2 tablespoons corn oil margarine
1 cup milk
2 egg yolks, slightly beaten
2 teaspoons baking powder
2 egg whites

Combine water and salt in a saucepan; bring to full rolling boil. Gradually add farina, stirring constantly, until mixture is well blended. Remove from heat. Mix in margarine, milk and egg yolks. Beat baking powder with egg whites, scraping bowl often, until mixture forms soft peaks when the beater is raised. Fold into farina mixture. Pour into greased 1½-quart casserole. Bake in 350°F. oven until center of spoon bread springs back when touched lightly, about 45 minutes. Serve at once. Makes 4 to 6 servings.

))•))

They may not drink buttermilk, but they'll certainly eat it! This bread will go together in minutes, and be eaten just as fast.

BUTTERMILK CHEDDAR CHEESE BREAD

3¾ cups packaged biscuit mix
¼ cup sugar
1½ cups shredded Cheddar cheese
1½ cups buttermilk
2 eggs, beaten

In a large bowl, combine biscuit mix and sugar. Add shredded cheese. Combine buttermilk and eggs; add to dry ingredients. Stir just until blended. Turn into a greased 9 x 5 x 3 inch loaf pan. Bake in a 350°F. oven 45 to 55 minutes, or until lightly browned. Loosen around the edges and turn out of pan onto a wire rack to cool. Makes 8 servings.

〰〰

Here's a bread than can do double duty as a cake. It has all of your favorite dried fruits chopped up with complimentary seasonings, and then used as a filling for a wrapping of dough.

FRUIT BREAD

1¼ cups dried apricots
1½ cups dried prunes
2 dried figs
1½ cups raisins
1 cup chopped walnuts
⅓ cup sugar
1 tablespoon ground cinnamon
Dash ground nutmeg
Dash ground cloves
2¼ cups sifted flour
½ teaspoon salt

½ cup corn oil margarine
¼ cup water
1 egg yolk, slightly beaten

Cover apricots, prunes and figs with water in a saucepan; cook over low heat for 15 minutes. Remove from heat and cool to room temperature. Drain. Pit prunes and put plumped fruit through a food chopper, using a medium blade. Mix together the fruit mixture, raisins, walnuts, sugar, cinnamon, nutmeg, and cloves. Mix flour and salt in a mixing bowl. Cut in margarine with a pastry blender or 2 knives until mixture is well mixed and forms fine crumbs. Sprinkle water over mixture while tossing to blend. Press dough firmly into a ball with your hands. Roll out between two pieces of waxed paper to a rectangle about 16 x 13 inches. Remove top piece of waxed paper. Place fruit mixture in compact row lengthwise down the center of dough, about 2½ inches from ends. Moisten edges of dough with a little water, then fold sides around fruit mixture, sealing together on top. Fold up ends; seal. Roll over onto ungreased baking sheet so center seam is down. Prick with fork; brush with egg yolk. Bake in 375°F. oven for 1 hour or until golden brown. Cool and slice. Makes about 15 slices.

)⟩✦⟩)

These back-to-nature ingredients would make a health food store owner proud. All combine to make bread that's good tasting and good for you too!

PRUNE–NUT BREAD

2¼ cups sifted flour
1½ cups wheat germ

2 teaspoons baking powder
1 teaspoon baking soda
1½ teaspoons salt
½ cup corn oil margarine
1 cup pitted prunes, snipped
½ cup chopped walnuts
2 eggs
¾ cup honey
¾ cup milk

Combine flour, wheat germ, baking powder, baking soda and salt. Cut in margarine with a fork or pastry blender until the mixture looks like coarse oatmeal. Stir in prunes and nuts. Add eggs, one at a time, mixing well after each. Add honey and milk and combine well. Turn batter into a greased 8-inch square pan and bake in an oven preheated to 350°F. for 35 to 45 minutes, or until pick that is inserted in the center comes out clean. Cut in squares.

)❖)

Fresh cranberries are chopped with nuts and pineapple to make this unusual batter. Make it a day ahead of time, for best taste and slicing!

CRANBERRY–PINEAPPLE BREAD

2 cups sifted flour
1 cup sugar
1½ teaspoons baking powder
½ teaspoon baking soda
1 teaspoon salt
1 8-ounce can crushed pineapple
1 teaspoon grated lemon rind

2 tablespoons melted margarine
1 egg, well beaten
½ cup chopped nuts
1½ cups fresh cranberries, coarsely chopped

Sift together the flour, sugar, baking powder, baking soda and salt. Drain off 2 tablespoons of liquid from the can of crushed pineapple and discard. Combine the remaining pineapple and juice with lemon rind, melted margarine and beaten egg. Stir mixture into the dry ingredients just until the dry ingredients are dampened. Fold in the chopped nuts and cranberries. Pour into a greased 9 x 5 x 3 inch pan. Push batter into the corners of the pan leaving the center slightly lower. Bake in a 350°F. oven for 60 minutes, or until an inserted toothpick comes out clean. Remove from pan and cool. Wrap in foil and store overnight for best flavor and easy slicing. Makes 8 servings.

)⸱⸱)

Here's a healthier recipe to make bran muffins the unsaturated fat way. Skim milk and vegetable shortening join all-bran cereal for maximum flavor and health!

BRAN MUFFINS

1½ cups sifted flour
1 tablespoon baking powder
1 teaspoon salt
½ cup sugar
1½ cups all-bran cereal
1 cup skim milk
1 egg
⅓ cup vegetable shortening, softened

Sift together the flour, baking powder, salt, and sugar; set aside. Stir together the all-bran cereal and milk; let stand for several minutes until most of the liquid is absorbed by the cereal. Then add egg and vegetable shortening and beat well. Stir in the flour mixture only until well combined. Fill a greased muffin pan (having twelve 2½-inch muffin cups) until ¾ full. Bake in a 400°F. oven for about 25 minutes, or until muffins are golden brown. Makes 12 muffins.

)•)

The beaten egg whites will give you a better textured muffin. Be sure to fold it in rather than stir and break up the air bubbles!

CORN MUFFINS

¼ cup corn oil margarine
¼ cup sugar
2 eggs, separated
1 cup skim milk
1 cup cornmeal
1 cup flour
4 teaspoons baking powder
½ teaspoon salt

Cream the margarine and sugar together. Beat in egg yolks. Add skim milk. Sift corn meal, flour, baking powder, and salt together. Beat egg whites until stiff. Add dry ingredients to the egg yolk batter, stirring well. Then fold in the beaten egg whites. Spoon into greased muffin tins. Makes 12 muffins.

)•)

These go together in minutes and are a flavorsome change. If your supermarket doesn't carry graham flour, try your nearest health food store!

GRAHAM MUFFINS

1 cup graham flour
1 cup regular flour
2 tablespoons sugar
4 teaspoons baking powder
½ teaspoon salt
1¼ cups skim milk
1 egg
4 tablespoons melted corn oil margarine

Sift graham flour, regular flour, sugar, baking powder, and salt together; stir to distribute the ingredients evenly. Beat milk, egg, and melted margarine together; stir into dry ingredients. Pour into greased muffin cups and bake in a 350°F. oven for 25 minutes, or until lightly browned. Makes 12 muffins.

))◦))

Easier than making rye bread, and much the same taste! You'll find caraway seeds on the herb and spice shelves of your local market.

RYE MUFFINS

1 cup flour
1 cup rye flour
4 teaspoons baking powder
¼ cup sugar
1 teaspoon salt

1 teaspoon caraway seeds
1 cup skim milk
1 egg

Sift regular flour, rye flour, baking powder, sugar and salt together; stir to distribute ingredients evenly. Add caraway seeds. Beat milk and egg together; add to dry ingredients. Beat well. Pour batter into greased muffin tins and bake at 350°F. for 25 minutes, or until lightly browned. Makes 12 muffins.

)❖)

Hot biscuits go with chicken dinner. Mmmmmm! If you haven't a biscuit cutter, use the floured rim of a juice glass.

BISCUITS

2 cups sifted flour
3 teaspoons baking powder
1 teaspoon salt
4 tablespoons vegetable shortening
¾ cup skim milk

Sift flour, baking powder, and salt together. Cut in shortening. Add milk to make a soft dough. Turn out on a floured board and knead for half a minute. Then roll out to ½-inch thickness and cut with a floured biscuit cutter. Bake on an ungreased baking sheet in a 450°F. oven for 10 to 12 minutes. Makes 1 dozen.

)❖)

Instead of a recipe for the bread itself, here's one for the tasty filling of an Israeli taco. It's an interesting departure from the usual hamburger!

ISRAELI TACO

1 15½-ounce can garbanzo beans, drained and washed in
  cold water
1 garlic clove, finely chopped
1 tablespoon lemon juice
¼ teaspoon coriander
¼ teaspoon salt
¼ teaspoon cayenne
2 rounds of Middle Eastern bread

Mix the garbanzos in a large bowl with garlic, lemon juice, coriander, salt, and cayenne. Let stand for half an hour until mixture is well blended. Cut or tear Middle Eastern bread in half to form two envelopes. Spoon garbanzo mixture into envelopes. Makes 4 servings.

12. Satisfying Desserts

))•)❖

It's the sweet tooth that usually trips up the best intended change in eating! Here's a treasury of recipes to keep you on the track to healthier Jewish cookery. That special tooth will tingle with delight at every bite!

))•))

Put applesauce, fruit, and coconut together and what have you got? A dessert ambrosia!

APPLE AMBROSIA

2 cups canned applesauce
1 banana, cut in slices
1 cup fresh cherries, pitted and halved
2 seedless oranges, cut in segments
1 teaspoon sugar
1 tablespoon lemon juice
¼ cup grated coconut

Combine applesauce, banana slices, cherry halves, and orange segments. Sprinkle with sugar and lemon juice. Stir. Spoon into dessert glasses and top with a sprinkling of coconut. Chill. Makes 6 servings.

)❖)

Another way to raise applesauce into the realm of the unusual. Combine it with yoghurt and other goodies and pile into tall stemmed glasses!

APPLE NUT FLUFF

1 cup applesauce
1 cup vanilla flavored yoghurt
¼ cup seedless raisins
¼ cup chopped walnuts
¼ cup shredded coconut

Combine applesauce and yoghurt, mixing well. Add raisins and nuts. Spoon into 6 dessert dishes. Sprinkle with coconut. Chill. Makes 6 servings.

)❖)

Beat the yoghurt before you stir in the pear syrup, and you'll have a fluffier topping. Fascinating how the simplest ingredients can combine to make an elegant dessert!

PEARS ELEGANT

1 29-ounce can pear halves
½ cup raspberry yoghurt
2 tablespoons finely chopped almonds

Drain pear halves and reserve the syrup. Arrange pears in dessert dishes. Stir 4 tablespoons of the reserved pear syrup into the raspberry yoghurt; mix well. Spoon over pears. Garnish with chopped almonds. Makes 6 to 8 servings.

〗◇〗

This recipe is intended for those calorie-counters who would rather use an artificial sweetener than skip dessert. Nobody will guess it's dietetic if you don't spill the beans!

APRICOT BRANDY DIET DESSERT

2 envelopes (2 tablespoons) unflavored gelatin
½ cup cold water
¾ cup boiling water
⅔ cup non-fat dry milk solids
1 tablespoon liquid non-nutritive sweetener
1 tablespoon imitation brandy flavoring
1 cup diced dietetic packed apricots, drained
6 ice cubes

Sprinkle gelatin over cold water in a 5-cup blender container and allow to soften while assembling other ingredients. Pour boiling water into blender. Cover; process at low speed until gelatin is dissolved. If gelatin granules cling to container, use a rubber spatula to push them into mixture. Add non-fat dry milk, non-nutritive sweetener and brandy flavoring. Process at low speed until well blended. Add ice cubes, one at a time, and process at high speed until ice is melted. Pour into sherbet glasses or compotes and chill. Makes 5 servings.

〗◇〗

Be sure to turn the cake pan over to cool before removing from the pan. A good way to do it is to slide the tube hole over an empty soda bottle, suspending it in the air to cool. This prevents the cake from "falling" as it would if left right-side-up. A cook's trick worth knowing!

LEMON FILLED LEMON CHIFFON CAKE

2¼ cups cake flour
1 cup sugar
1 tablespoon baking powder
1 teaspoon salt
½ cup salad oil
5 egg yolks
¾ cup cold water
2 teaspoons grated lemon rind
2 teaspoons vanilla extract
7 egg whites (use remaining 2 yolks for filling)
½ teaspoon cream of tartar
½ cup sugar
Lemon filling

Combine flour, 1 cup sugar, baking powder and salt in a large mixing bowl. Make a "well" in center of dry ingredients; add oil, egg yolks, water, lemon rind and vanilla. Beat until smooth. Beat egg whites with cream of tartar until soft peaks form; gradually add ½ cup sugar, beating constantly until egg whites stand in stiff glossy peaks. Pour egg yolk mixture over egg whites, a little at a time, folding in after each addition. Mix only until blended. Turn into ungreased 10-inch tube pan. Bake in a 325°F. oven for 60 to 70 minutes, or until cake springs back when lightly touched. Invert pan and cool cake thoroughly before removing from pan. Cut into three equal layers. Spread top of each layer with ⅓ of the Lemon Filling. Makes 12 to 16 servings.

Lemon Filling:
1 cup sugar
3 tablespoons cornstarch
Dash salt
1 cup cold water
2 egg yolks, slightly beaten
2 teaspoons grated lemon rind
¼ cup lemon juice
1 tablespoon corn oil margarine

Combine sugar, cornstarch and salt in saucepan; gradually stir in water. Blend in egg yolks, lemon rind and juice. Cook over medium heat, stirring constantly until mixture boils. Boil one minute, stirring constantly. Remove from heat and blend in margarine. Cool to room temperature without stirring. Use as filling for Lemon Chiffon Cake above.

))✧))

This is a most unusual sponge cake recipe. It combines the best of a spice cake with the lightness of a sponge. The Fluffy Peach Frosting on page 159 is a perfect complement!

SPICE SPONGE CAKE

1¼ cups sifted cake flour
¼ cup sugar
¼ teaspoon salt
1 teaspoon cinnamon
½ teaspoon allspice
½ teaspoon nutmeg
1 teaspoon cream of tartar
5 eggs, separated

¼ cup sugar
¾ cup dark corn syrup
½ teaspoon vanilla
½ teaspoon lemon extract

Sift together flour, ¼ cup sugar, salt, cinnamon, allspice and nutmeg three times. Add cream of tartar to egg whites and beat until slightly mounded when beater is raised; gradually beat in remaining ¼ cup sugar; slowly add corn syrup and continue beating until whites stand in firm peaks when beater is raised. Beat egg yolks until thick and lemon colored. Beat in vanilla and lemon extract. Fold egg yolks into egg white mixture. Gradually fold in dry ingredients, sifting about ¼ cup at a time over surface. Turn into ungreased 10 x 4 inch tube pan. Cut through with spatula to remove large bubbles. Bake in 325°F. oven for 50 to 55 minutes or until cake is lightly browned. Invert pan and let cake stand about 1 hour or until cool. To remove from pan, loosen side with spatula. Serves 12 to 14. Serve with Fluffy Peach Frosting, below, if desired.

))✦))

Beat egg whites first as if for meringue. Then add the other ingredients for a fabulous fluffy frosting!

FLUFFY PEACH FROSTING

2 egg whites
⅔ cup light corn syrup
½ cup peach preserves
1 teaspoon vanilla

Beat egg whites until stiff but not dry. Combine corn syrup and peach preserves. Gradually beat into egg whites, continuing to beat until frosting forms firm peaks when beater is raised. Fold in vanilla. Makes enough to cover tops and sides of two 8-inch layers, one 9-inch square or one 10-inch tube cake. To frost cake baked in a 1-quart ring mold, prepare half quantity.

)❖)

If you have never baked with yeast before, or you have and think it's too much bother for one cake, here's an easy and nourishing recipe for four Orange Coffee Cakes. One is for dinner and three go into your freezer bank, to make the whole project really worth your time and effort.

ORANGE COFFEE CAKE

1 6-ounce can frozen concentrated orange juice, thawed and undiluted
¼ cup corn oil margarine
½ cup honey
½ cup sugar
2 cakes compressed yeast
½ cup warm water
½ cup sugar
¼ cup vegetable shortening
1 teaspoon salt
1 cup boiling water
2 eggs
7 to 7½ cups sifted flour
¾ cup slivered almonds

In a small saucepan, combine ½ cup of the orange juice concentrate, margarine, honey and sugar. Cook over medium heat for 5 minutes, stirring frequently. Remove from heat; measure ⅛ cup of mixture into each of 4 baking pans.* Reserve remaining for topping.

Soften yeast in ½ cup warm water. In a large bowl, combine ½ cup sugar, shortening, salt, and boiling water; stir to melt shortening. Add cold water and remainder of orange juice concentrate. Cool to lukewarm.

Blend in unbeaten eggs and softened yeast. Add flour gradually to form a stiff dough; mix well. Turn out on floured surface and knead lightly until no longer sticky. Let rest for 15 minutes. Then divide dough into 4 equal parts. Divide each of those 4 parts into 6 pieces; then roll each piece to a 7-inch strip. Twist these strips slightly and place side by side in the prepared pans, parallel to the shortest side of the pan. Repeat this process for the other 3 coffee cakes. Cover lightly and let rise in a warm place until light and doubled in bulk. Drizzle remaining topping mixture over tops of coffee cakes and sprinkle with slivered almonds. Bake at 375°F. for 25 to 30 minutes, until golden brown. Cool.

* Use 4 aluminum foil baking pans, 8¾ x 5¾ x 1¼ inches, OR use one 8-inch square cake pan and one 13 x 9 inch pan for two larger coffee cakes.

)❖))

Tiny flecks of chocolate bake right in the cake for an unusual appearance and taste. Note that bread crumbs are used instead of flour. Invert pan as directed for Lemon Chiffon Cake on page 157.

CHOCOLATE FLAKE CAKE

6 eggs, separated
1 cup sugar

⅔ cup corn oil
1 teaspoon vanilla
1½ cups fine dry bread crumbs
2 teaspoons baking powder
¼ teaspoon salt
3 1-ounce squares semi-sweet baking chocolate, grated

Beat egg whites in a large mixing bowl until foamy. Gradually add ¼ cup sugar beating until soft peaks form when beater is raised. Set aside. Beat egg yolks in a large bowl until thick and lemon colored. Gradually beat in the remaining ¾ cup sugar, corn oil and vanilla. Mix together bread crumbs, baking powder, salt, and grated chocolate. Stir into egg yolk mixture, then fold into egg white mixture. Turn into ungreased 9-inch tube pan. Bake in a 325°F. oven for 1 hour or until cake springs back when lightly touched. Immediately invert pan and cool. Makes 9-inch tube cake.

)❖)

Poppy seeds are more apt to be found on bread or rolls, but here they are used to flavor the cake. Boil as directed before proceeding with the recipe!

POPPY SEED CAKE

1½ cups poppy seeds
6 eggs, separated
1 cup sugar
⅔ cup corn oil
1 teaspoon vanilla
1½ cups fine dry bread crumbs
2 teaspoons baking powder
¼ teaspoon salt

Cover poppy seeds with water in a 2-quart saucepan. Heat to boiling and boil 30 minutes, stirring occasionally, adding more water if needed. Drain in fine sieve. Cool. Beat egg whites in a large mixing bowl until foamy. Gradually add ¼ cup sugar beating until soft peaks form when beater is raised. Set aside. Beat egg yolks in a large bowl until thick and lemon colored. Gradually beat in the remaining ¾ cup sugar, corn oil and vanilla. Stir in poppy seeds. Mix together bread crumbs, baking powder and salt. Stir into poppy seed mixture, then fold into egg white mixture. Turn into ungreased 9 x 3½ inch tube pan. Bake in 325°F. oven for 1 hour or until cake springs back when lightly touched. Immediately invert pan and cool. Makes 9-inch tube cake.

)◆)

You not only can serve this cake for tea, you put tea right into the cake! And if you like a bit of lemon, you'll find it in paper thin slices atop of all.

RUSSIAN TEA CAKE

2½ cups sifted flour
3 teaspoons baking powder
½ teaspoon salt
½ cup cold strong tea
¼ cup milk
⅔ cup corn oil margarine
1¼ cups sugar
2 eggs
1½ teaspoons grated lemon rind
½ cup orange marmalade
Paper thin lemon slices

Sugar
Maraschino cherry halves

Grease two 8-inch layer cake pans; line the bottoms with waxed paper. Sift flour, baking powder and salt together. Combine tea and milk. Set both mixtures aside. Blend margarine and sugar together; add eggs, one at a time, blending until smooth. Add lemon rind. Stir in sifted dry ingredients alternately with tea mixture, beginning and ending with dry ingredients and stirring until smooth after each addition. Pour into prepared cake pans. Bake in 375°F. oven until cake tests done, about 30 to 35 minutes. Cool. Spread top of each layer with orange marmalade. Stack one on top of the other. Dip lemon slices into sugar; decorate top of cake with these lemon slices and maraschino cherry halves. Makes one 8-inch layer cake.

)⊁)

Who could resist squares of applesauce cake stuffed with raisins and nuts? Just like mama used to make!

APPLESAUCE CAKE

2⅓ cups sifted flour
1 teaspoon ground cinnamon
½ teaspoon salt
½ teaspoon ground cloves
½ teaspoon ground nutmeg
⅔ cup corn oil margarine
1 cup sugar
1⅓ cups warm applesauce
1¼ teaspoons baking soda
⅓ cup raisins
⅓ cup chopped nuts

Grease a 9-inch square baking pan; line bottom with waxed paper and grease again. Sift together flour, cinnamon, salt, cloves and nutmeg. Mix margarine and sugar until blended. Stir in 2 tablespoons of the applesauce. Add baking soda to remaining applesauce in small bowl, stirring until mixture foams and looks bubbly. Stir into margarine mixture alternately with sifted dry ingredients, mixing until smooth after each addition. Pour into prepared pan. Bake in 350°F. oven 45 to 50 minutes or until cake springs back when touched. Cool in pan. Cut into 3-inch squares. Makes 9 servings.

))✧))

Another chance to get acquainted with a yeast dough. A nice warm place where it can rise is right over the pilot light on your range. Peanut butter sets the flavor!

PEANUT BUTTER COFFEE RING

½ cup skim milk
2 tablespoons corn oil margarine
2 tablespoons peanut butter
2 tablespoons sugar
½ teaspoon salt
1 package active dry yeast
¼ cup warm water
1 egg, beaten
1½ cups flour
1 recipe Glaze (below)
1 recipe Topping (below)

Heat milk, margarine, peanut butter, sugar and salt in a small saucepan over low heat until warm. Margarine does not have to melt. Dissolve yeast in warm water. Using a wooden spoon, beat peanut butter mixture with yeast, egg and flour in a mixing bowl for about 1 minute, or until smooth. Cover; let rise in a warm place, free from draft for about 1 hour or until doubled in bulk. Stir batter down. Turn into a greased 1-quart ring mold, spreading evenly. Cover, let rise in warm place about 20 minutes or until doubled in bulk. Bake in 375°F. oven about 30 minutes or until browned. Remove from pan immediately; cool. Cover top with Glaze, letting some run down the sides. Sprinkle with Topping. Makes 6 to 8 servings.

Sugar Glaze:
1 cup confectioners sugar
2 tablespoons water

   Mix sugar and water until smooth. Makes ½ cup.

Peanut Butter Topping:
3 tablespoons fine dry bread crumbs
2 tablespoons flour
1 tablespoon peanut butter
1 tablespoon corn oil margarine

   Mix bread crumbs and flour; cut in peanut butter and margarine with a fork until crumbs form. Makes ½ cup.

))•<))

   What could be better than an applesauce cake? An applesauce fruit cake, that's what!

APPLESAUCE FRUIT CAKE

2 cups applesauce
⅔ cup corn oil margarine
1⅛ cups sugar

2¾ cups flour
2½ teaspoons baking soda
1½ teaspoons cinnamon
½ teaspoon nutmeg
½ teaspoon salt
¼ teaspoon ground cloves
1¼ cups raisins
1 cup dates, cut up
1 cup nuts, coarsely chopped
½ cup candied cherries cut in halves
½ cup candied fruits and citrons

Combine the applesauce, margarine, and sugar in a saucepan and boil for 5 minutes. Remove from heat and chill in the refrigerator for 15 minutes. Meanwhile, sift the flour, soda, cinnamon, nutmeg, salt, cloves together into a large bowl. Add the raisins, dates, nuts and fruits and mix thoroughly with the dry ingredients. Add the chilled applesauce mixture and blend well. Pour the batter into a greased and floured tube pan. Bake at 275°F. for 2½ to 3 hours or until a toothpick inserted into the cake comes out clean. Makes one 2½-pound cake.

)❖)

Two kinds of jam fill the layers of this lovely almond torte. A no-cook frosting gives it an elegant finish!

ALMOND TORTE

2 cups sifted flour
1 teaspoon baking powder
½ teaspoon salt
1 cup corn oil margarine
1 cup sugar

3 eggs, separated
1 6-ounce can almonds, blanched and finely chopped
Grated rind and juice of 1 lemon
⅔ cup strawberry preserves
⅓ cup apricot preserves

Sift together flour, baking powder and salt. Cream margarine; add sugar and beat until light. Add egg yolks and mix well. Stir in almonds, lemon juice and rind. Add sifted dry ingredients and mix until well blended. Beat egg whites stiff; fold into batter. Turn into a greased jelly roll pan, 15½ x 10½ x 1 inches. Bake in a 350°F. oven for 25 to 30 minutes. When cake is cool, cut into quarters. Stack the four pieces of cake, spreading strawberry preserves between the top and bottom layers, and spreading apricot preserves between the middle layers. Frost with fluffy No-cook Frosting below and garnish with almonds if desired.

No-cook Frosting:
⅛ teaspoon salt
1 egg white
2 tablespoons sugar
⅓ cup light corn syrup
½ teaspoon vanilla

Add salt to egg white and beat until mixture forms soft peaks. Gradually add sugar, about 1 tablespoon at a time, beating until smooth and glossy. Continue beating and add light corn syrup, a little at a time, beating thoroughly after each addition, until frosting peaks. Fold in vanilla. Spread generously over top and sides of Almond Torte. Makes 8 servings.

)❖)

This sponge cake uses potato starch instead of flour. Ginger, nutmeg, and lemon give it a most gladdening aroma!

PASSOVER SPONGE CAKE

6 eggs, separated
1½ cups sugar
1½ tablespoons lemon juice
1 teaspoon grated fresh lemon peel
¾ cup sifted potato starch
¼ teaspoon salt
¼ teaspoon ground ginger
¼ teaspoon ground nutmeg

Beat egg yolks until lemon colored. Gradually beat in sugar. Add lemon juice and peel. Sift potato starch with salt, ginger and nutmeg; gradualy add it to the batter. Beat egg whites until stiff peaks form; fold into the batter carefully so batter will retain its spongy nature while you are combining the mixtures. Pour batter into a tube pan and bake in a 350°F. preheated oven for 1 hour, or until cake is firm. Remove from oven and turn pan over to cool. Top with sifted confectioners' sugar, if desired. Makes 12 to 14 servings.

꙳

This is just the kind of cake that old-fashioned mamas used to make. Serve it warm for a delightfully different taste!

APPLE STREUSEL CAKE

½ cup flour
¾ cup sugar

1 tablespoon baking powder
⅛ teaspoon salt
¼ cup margarine
1 egg
½ cup milk
1 teaspoon vanilla
2 large baking apples, peeled, cored, and sliced
2 tablespoons lemon juice
¼ cup brown sugar
1 tablespoon flour
1 teaspoon cinnamon
1 tablespoon melted margarine
¼ cup chopped almonds

Sift the flour, sugar, baking powder and salt together into a deep bowl. Cut in margarine with two knives or a pastry blender until the mixture is crumbly. Beat the egg, milk, and vanilla together; add to the flour mixture. Grease and flour a flat 6 x 10 inch pan; spread half the batter over the bottom of the pan. Sprinkle apple slices with lemon juice and arrange them neatly over the batter. Then pour the remaining batter over the apples. Combine the brown sugar, flour and cinnamon; stir in the melted margarine and then the nuts. Sprinkle this mixture over the top of the batter and bake in a 375°F. oven for 30 minutes, or until firm and lightly browned. Cut in squares. Makes 8 to 10 servings.

)•◆)

No need to buy special cakes for Passover. Bake your own! Here's an easy recipe to get you started.

PASSOVER NUT CAKE

6 eggs, separated
1 cup sugar
½ cup matzo meal
½ teaspoon salt
½ pound chopped wanuts

Beat yolks until lemon colored. Gradually beat in the sugar. Then add matzo meal, salt, and chopped nuts. Beat egg whites until stiff. Fold into batter. Pour into a 9-inch square pan and bake in a 350°F. oven for 35 to 40 minutes. Cut in squares. Makes 9 servings.

Breathes there a heathier cheesecake, free of fatty cream? Yes, and here it is topped with applesauce to make it extra good!

CHEESECAKE WITH APPLE TOPPING

1 cup skim milk
4 eggs
2 envelopes unflavored gelatin
1 cup sugar
1 teaspoon vanilla
2 pounds cream-style cottage cheese, sieved or blended

Pour milk into top of double boiler. Beat in eggs until well combined. Mix gelatin and sugar, stir into milk-egg mixture. Cook over boiling water, stirring constantly, until gelatin is dissolved and mixture has thickened, 10 to 15 minutes. Remove from heat and cool slightly. Stir vanilla into sieved cottage cheese; mix well. Stir in custard mixture; mix well. Pour into 8-inch springform pan. Chill until almost firm. Cover with Apple Topping below. Chill at least 1 hour longer. At serving time, remove side of pan and place cheesecake on serving platter. Makes 10 to 12 servings.

Apple Topping:
1 15-ounce jar applesauce
1 teaspoon cornstarch
½ teaspoon cinnamon

Pour about ¼ cup applesauce into a saucepan. Stir in cornstarch until smooth. Stir in rest of applesauce and cinnamon. Cook over a medium heat, stirring constantly until mixture comes to a boil. Cool. Spoon over top of cheesecake.

)❖)

You'll wonder why you didn't double the recipe for strudel when you watch it disappear. It's the kind of a dessert you remember!

RAISIN–NUT STRUDEL

2 eggs
4 tablespoons corn oil
1¼ cups flour
1 tablespoon baking powder
1 teaspoon salt
1 cup strawberry jam
1 cup raisins
1 cup finely chopped walnuts

1 tablespoon sugar
½ teaspoon cinnamon

Beat eggs; then beat in 3 tablespoons of the corn oil one tablespoon at a time. Combine flour, baking powder, and salt. Stir into egg mixture and then knead into a soft dough. Roll out into a thin rectangle. Combine jam, raisins, walnuts, sugar, and cinnamon; spread over entire surface of the dough. Roll dough, starting at one end (long side), jelly-roll fashion. Place on a greased cookie sheet. Brush with remaining tablespoon of corn oil. Bake in a 350°F. oven for 1 hour, or until lighty browned. Cool and then slice. Makes 8 to 10 servings.

)➔)

The healthier way to make pie crust is with a vegetable margarine or bland tasting oil. This one is especially easy to handle—even if you've always had trouble with crusts!

OIL PASTRY

Single Crust Pie:
1⅓ cups sifted flour
½ teaspoon salt
⅓ cup corn oil
2 tablespoons cold water

Mix the flour and salt in a bowl. Add corn oil, mixing thoroughly with a fork. Sprinkle all water on top; then mix well. Press firmly into a ball with your hands. (If slightly dry, mix in 1 to 2 tablespoons additional corn oil.) Flatten dough slightly, and immediately roll out to 12-inch circle between 2 pieces of waxed paper. (Wipe table with a

damp cloth to keep paper from slipping.) Peel off top
paper; place in a 9-inch pie pan, paper side up. Peel off
paper; fit pastry loosely into pan. Trim dough ½ inch beyond rim of pan, if necessary. Flute edge. If shell is to be
baked before filling, prick thoroughly and bake in 450°F.
oven 12 to 15 minutes or until golden brown. If shell and
filling are to be baked together, do not prick shell; bake
pie according to filling used.

Double Crust Pie:
2 cups sifted flour
1 teaspoon salt
½ cup corn oil
3 tablespoons cold water

Mix flour and salt in a bowl. Add corn oil, mixing thoroughly with a fork. Sprinkle all water on top; mix well.
Press firmly into a ball with your hands. (If slightly dry,
mix in 1 to 2 tablespoons additional corn oil.) Divide dough
almost in half. Flatten larger portion slightly; roll out to
12-inch circle between 2 pieces of waxed paper. Peel off
top paper; place dough in a 9-inch pie pan, paper side up.
Peel off paper; fit pastry loosely into pan. Fill as desired.
Trim dough ½ inch beyond rim of pan, if necessary. Roll
out remaining dough for top crust. Peel off paper, cut slits
to permit steam to escape during baking and place over
filling. Trim ½ inch beyond rim of pan. Fold edges of both
crusts under; seal and flute. Bake pie according to filling
used.

)◊)

Be sure to bake and cool the pie crust before you begin
to make the pie. This tastes like chiffon pie, only better!

RASPBERRY YOGHURT PIE

1 3-ounce package raspberry gelatin
1 cup boiling water
1 8-ounce can crushed pineapple
1 8-ounce container raspberry yoghurt
1 9-inch baked pie crust

Empty raspberry gelatin into a bowl and mix with boiling water until completely dissolved. Drain liquid from pineapple into a cup and add water until it measures ¾ cup of liquid; stir into gelatin. Chill until slightly thickened (to the consistency of egg whites), and then add pineapple and stirred-up yoghurt. Mix well and pour into pie crust. Return to refrigerator and chill for several hours. Serve with non-dairy whipped topping, if desired. Makes 6 servings.

))✦))

If you use self-rising cake flour, omit the baking powder and salt. Then proceed to fill with orange flavored Lekvar!

HAMANTASCHEN #1

Cookie Dough:
5 cups sifted cake flour
2 tablespoons baking powder
1 teaspoon salt
4 eggs, slightly beaten
¾ cup corn oil
¾ cup sugar

Filling:
3 cups Lekvar
3 tablespoons grated orange rind

Sift flour, baking powder and salt together; set aside. Combine eggs, corn oil, and sugar. Beat until the mixture is fluffy and thick. Gently stir in flour mixture. Chill about 1½ hours or until dough is firm. Then divide dough into quarters. Roll out each quarter on a floured board or cloth to ⅛-inch thickness. Cut into 2½ or 3 inch circles and place on greased baking sheet. Combine Lekvar and orange rind. Spoon 1 tablespoon of this mixture into the center of each circle; form tricorns by bringing up the edges of the dough almost to the center and making 3 seams. (Some filling should show in center.) Pinch seams together tightly. Bake in a 350°F. oven for 15 to 20 minutes or until golden brown. Makes about 4 dozen 3-inch cookies or 6 dozen 2½-inch cookies.

꒰꓄꒱

Perhaps you will prefer this version with margarine instead of corn oil used in the preceding recipe. The filling is different too—combining prunes with honey, lemon, and almonds!

HAMANTASCHEN #2

Cookie Dough:
¾ cup sugar
2 cups flour
1½ teaspoons baking powder
¼ teaspoon salt
½ cup margarine
1 egg, beaten
2 tablespoons orange juice

Filling:
1 15-ounce jar cooked prunes, drained
½ cup honey

2 tablespoons lemon juice
Grated rind of 1 lemon
¼ cup ground almonds

Sift sugar, flour, baking powder and salt into a mixing bowl. Work in the margarine with your fingertips or a pastry blender. Combine egg and orange juice, stir in to make a firm dough. Chill well before rolling out. Roll dough on a lightly floured board to ⅛-inch thickness. Cut out 3-inch rounds. Put a tablespoon of prune filling in the center of each round. Bring the edges together to form a triangle, pinching them to seal. Leave a small opening in the center, or at each corner. Bake on greased baking sheet in a 400°F. oven for 12 minutes, until golden brown. Makes 2 dozen.

To make prune filling: Pit the prunes, chop, and put into a small sauce pan with honey and lemon juice. (Use the drained prune syrup mixed with apple juice for a refreshing drink.) Bring to a boil and simmer, stirring often, until the mixture is thick. Remove from heat. Stir in lemon rind and nuts. Cool before using to fill Hamantaschen.

)❖)

These are the dark delicious cookies that look so fragile and cool so quickly! Makes enough for everyone to have a party!

LACE WAFERS

1 cup sifted flour
1 cup chopped nuts
½ cup dark corn syrup
½ cup firmly packed brown sugar
½ cup corn oil margarine
1 teaspoon vanilla

Mix sifted flour and nuts. Combine corn syrup, brown sugar and margarine in a heavy saucepan; bring to a boil over medium heat, stirring constantly. Remove from heat. Gradually blend in the flour-nut mixture, then stir in vanilla. Drop batter onto foil-covered cooky sheet by scant teaspoonfuls, 3 inches apart. Bake in 350°F. oven for 8 to 10 minutes. Cool on wire rack until foil may easily be peeled off, 3 to 4 minutes. Remove foil; cool cookies on wire rack covered with absorbent paper. Makes 4½ dozen cookies.

※※

Peanut butter, dates and coconut are combined in these cookies for a healthy mouthful. Fill some with jelly as directed and it will look as though you were baking two different kinds. Kitchen trickery!

DATE–NUT COOKIES

2 eggs
½ cup sugar
1 teaspoon vanilla
½ teaspoon salt
¾ cup peanut butter
½ cup chopped dates
½ cup flaked coconut

Beat eggs in a mixing bowl with rotary beater until thick and lemon colored. Stir in sugar, vanilla and salt. Add peanut butter, dates and coconut; mix well. Chill for 2 to 3 hours. Drop by teaspoonfuls onto a greased cooky sheet. Flatten with a fork, making crosswise pattern on each cookie. Bake in 300°F. oven until cookies are lightly browned, about 25 minutes. Makes 2½ dozen cookies.

To Make Jelly Filled Cookies: Follow directions above, but instead of making a fork design, make a slight indentation in the center of each cookie with the back of a spoon. Bake in 300°F. oven for 20 minutes. Remove and fill the centers with jelly; then bake cookies until lightly browned, about 5 minutes more.

〉〉◊〉〉

Who ever heard of mayonnaise and honey in a brownie recipe? You did—right here! Fantastic!

BITTERSWEET BROWNIES

1½ cups (9 ounces) semi-sweet chocolate pieces
¼ cup corn oil margarine
2 eggs
⅓ cup honey
½ cup mayonnaise
1 teaspoon vanilla
½ cup sifted flour
½ teaspoon baking powder
½ cup coarsely chopped pecans or walnuts

Grease a 9-inch square baking pan. Melt chocolate pieces and margarine in a small saucepan over low heat; stir constantly. Cool. Beat eggs in a large mixing bowl. Gradually add honey and mix well. Add mayonnaise, chocolate mixture, and vanilla; beat well. Sift together flour and baking powder; stir into chocolate mixture. Mix in nuts. Turn into the greased baking pan. Bake in 350°F. oven for 30 minutes, or until cake tester inserted in center comes out clean. Cool and cut into 2¼-inch squares. Makes 16 brownies.

〉〉◊〉〉

Brownies do not have to be made of chocolate. These are made with good old reliable peanut butter and numerous other nice things!

PEANUT BUTTER BROWNIES

½ cup peanut butter
⅓ cup corn oil margarine
⅔ cup sugar
½ cup firmly packed dark brown sugar
2 eggs
½ teaspoon almond extract
1 cup flour
1 teaspoon baking powder
¼ teaspoon salt

Grease a 9-inch square baking pan. Mix peanut butter and margarine. Gradually add sugars, beating until fluffy. Beat in eggs, one at a time, then almond extract until well mixed. Stir together flour, baking powder and salt. Stir into peanut butter mixture until well blended. Turn into prepared pan. Bake in 350°F. oven for 30 to 35 minutes or until cake springs back when touched lightly. Cool. Cut into 16 squares.

)❖))

Top with coffee ice cream for a taste that can't be beat. Cut in smaller bars for pick-up serving!

PRUNE BARS

½ cup flour
½ teaspoon baking powder
½ teaspoon salt

2 eggs
½ cup sugar
½ teaspoon vanilla
1 cup pitted prunes, chopped
1 cup chopped walnuts

Sift together flour, baking powder and salt. Set aside. Beat eggs and gradually beat in sugar. Add vanilla. Stir in flour mixture, reserving about ¼ cup to mix with the chopped prunes and nuts; stir this into the batter also. Pour into a 9-inch square greased baking pan. Bake in a 325°F. oven for 30 minutes. Cut into 12 servings.

)►◄)

If you flour your hands lightly before forming the chilled dough into balls, it will be easier to do. Be careful not to overbake these!

PEANUT BUTTER COOKIES

1⅔ cups sifted flour
1½ teaspoons baking powder
⅛ teaspoon salt
½ cup corn oil margarine
½ cup firmly packed brown sugar
½ cup creamy peanut butter
⅓ cup dark corn syrup
1 egg
½ teaspoon vanilla
Additional peanut butter, optional

Sift flour, baking powder and salt together. Blend margarine and sugar. Blend in ½ cup peanut butter and corn syrup until smooth. Beat in egg and vanilla. Gradually mix in dry ingredients, mixing well after each addition. Chill several hours or until dough is easy to handle. Roll dough into 1-inch balls. Place on ungreased baking sheet. Flatten with floured fork. If desired, place about ½ teaspoon additional peanut butter on top of each cookie. Bake in a 350°F. oven for 12 to 15 minutes or until set but not hard. Makes 3½ dozen cookies.

)⊹)

This has the classical taste of the traditional recipe, and is shaped much the same way now as then. Form into a long flat loaf with rounded ends as directed, cut while hot, and rebake to crisp. A taste of the past!

MANDEL BRODT

2 eggs
½ cup sugar
Grated rind of ½ lemon
½ teaspoon vanilla
1⅔ cups flour
¼ cup corn oil
¼ cup finely chopped almonds
2 teaspoons baking powder

Beat eggs well. Gradually add sugar. Add lemon rind and vanilla. Beat in 1 cup of the flour. Add oil. Stir remaining flour, almonds, and baking powder together and add to batter. You will now have a soft dough. Flour hands and shape dough into a long flat loaf with rounded ends, about 3 inches wide and 1 inch high. Place on a greased cookie sheet and bake in a 350°F. oven for 40 to 45 minutes, or until lightly browned. Remove from oven and cut into half-inch slices. Return to oven for 10 minutes to crisp slices. Makes about 2 dozen pieces.

)❧)

These cinnamon flavored raisin cookies are a Passover cookie jar treat, but you'll be baking them all year. They're that good!

MATZO MEAL RAISIN COOKIES

½ cup corn oil margarine
1½ cups sugar
4 eggs
2 cups matzo meal
2 cups matzo farfel
1 teaspoon cinnamon
1 cup seedless raisins

Beat margarine and sugar together until fluffy. Add eggs, one at a time, and beat well. Combine matzo meal, matzo farfel, and cinnamon. Gradually stir into the batter. Stir in raisins. Drop by heaping teaspoonfuls onto a greased cookie sheet and bake at 350°F. for 20 to 25 minutes, or until lightly browned. Makes about 3 dozen cookies.

)❧)

Another Passover cookie that whips up in a jiffy. Add some chocolate bits to half the batter for a novelty now and again!

COCONUT MACAROONS

2 egg whites
Dash salt

½ teaspoon vanilla
⅔ cup sugar
1 cup flaked coconut

Beat egg whites until foamy. Add salt and vanilla and continue beating. Add sugar gradually and continue beating until egg whites are stiff. Fold in coconut. Drop by rounded teaspoons onto greased cookie sheet. Bake in a 325°F. oven for 20 minutes. Makes about 2 dozen cookies.

)✧)

Serve this prune-apple pancake sauce with potato pancakes on page 123, for a mini-course or maxi-dessert! Terrific!

PRUNE–APPLE PANCAKE SAUCE

1 cup pitted prunes
2 cups applesauce
⅛ teaspoon cinnamon
Dash of nutmeg

Cut pitted prunes into small slivers and combine with the applesauce. Stir in cinnamon and nutmeg. Serve with potato pancakes. Makes 3 cups of sauce.

)✧)

If you're wondering what to do with fresh strawberries, blueberries, or sliced peaches—make these shortcakes and fill between the layers and on top. A spritz of lo-cal whipped topping adds a tasty touch!

EXTRA–RICH SHORTCAKE

2 cups sifted flour
3 teaspoons baking powder
2 tablespoons sugar
1 teaspoon salt
1 egg
⅓ cup corn oil
Milk

Mix and sift dry ingredients together. Add egg to corn oil in measuring cup. Pour in milk to make 1 cup total liquid. Then pour all at once over entire surface of flour mixture. Mix with fork to make a soft dough. Shape lightly with hands to make a round ball. Place on waxed paper and knead lightly ten times or until smooth. Pat out a ½-inch thickness or roll between 2 squares waxed paper (about 12 inches square). Remove top sheet of paper; cut shortcakes with unfloured 2½-inch cutter. Place on ungreased baking sheet. Bake in 450°F. oven for 12 to 15 minutes. Split shortcakes with a fork, while still warm. Spread fruit between layers and on top. Serve warm with whipped topping, if desired. Makes 8 shortcakes.

))✦))

Index